getting deep

Understand **what** you believe about God and **why**

 TruthQuest

getting deep

Understand
what you
believe about
God and **why**

GREGG R. ALLISON

BROADMAN
&HOLMAN
PUBLISHERS

NASHVILLE, TENNESSEE

Published by Broadman & Holman Publishers,
Nashville, Tennessee

Subject Heading: YOUTH / CHRISTIAN LIVING

1 2 3 4 5 6 7 8 9 10 06 05 04 03 02

Contents

About . . .

You

High school student who loves God. Serious about your faith in Jesus Christ. Or at least interested and willing to explore Christianity. Tired of fluff and pat answers. Challenged by deeper level discussions. Including deep theology (see below). Not afraid to wrestle with an issue, put it down, then come back and have another go at it. But not with theory; it has to work, has to make a difference. Certain that in this mysterious reality that we call human existence, a sure and true Word from God is given to shed enough light to shape our experience in a way that we can know God and please him.

Me

Dad to three students—one in college, another in high school, a third bringing up the rear. Husband of *the best* woman. At church, I worship God and have fun by directing the board, teaching Sunday school, working through tough issues, and hanging out with friends. Teacher of theology (see below). Been a pastor, missionary, college minister, soccer coach (little kids), baseball coach (Little Leaguers), and editor. Cubs fan, Bulls fan, Bears fan (formerly from Chicago). I love God and students.

God

The subject of this book. The ONLY subject. In fact, the subject of everything that exists. "For in Him we live and move and exist"

(Acts 17:28). That includes you and me. There is nothing more important than God.

Theology

The study of God based on what he reveals about himself in the entire Bible. Carefully organized by topics and clearly communicated so as to be understood and lived out concretely. Sometimes these topics are referred to as *doctrines*. A *doctrine* is a truth that is based on what the Bible affirms, and it impacts us in a life-changing way. We could also refer to these topics or doctrines as *beliefs*. A *belief* is a truth that is commonly held by Christians, not only by those who are living, but also by those who have been part of the Christian church over the course of its two-thousand-year existence. Beliefs are also based on the teaching of the Bible, and they influence not only what we think but our entire lives as well. Because this book is part of the *TruthQuest* series, we can also call these crucial topics *truths*. A *truth* is a sure idea that corresponds to reality. To say that the walls of my office are painted white is a truth; to say that they are green or red is an error. The truths we will explore in this book come from the Bible. When we become convinced of them—and I urge you to develop a strong sense of certainty about them—they change our lives. Doctrines, beliefs, truths—these are the focus of theology.

This Book

About you, me, God, and theology. This book covers a lot of material about God. In one sense, we could spend our entire lives speaking about him and never come to an end. In another sense, though, certain doctrines (or beliefs or truths) will help you to go deeper with God, and it is these on which I will focus. I will turn to key passages of Scripture in my writing and help you to understand what they tell us about God. I also will write about God from the perspective of what the entire Bible teaches us about him. So, though I focus on certain key parts of Scripture, I want you to know that those key passages are considered in light of what the whole Bible affirms about God. Also, I will tell you something about myself through stories about my experience of God. In return, I hope you will go deeper with God and experience him in a powerful new way. To encourage this, I will give you questions to wonder about and suggest activities you can do. As God, you, and I join together in this process, we'll do some great theology!

Chocolate Malts and the God Question

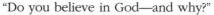

CHAPTER 1

"Do you believe in God—and why?"

One eighteen-year-old student posed the question, but everyone seated around the table nodded in agreement. This was the issue the group wanted to discuss.

A Sunday school class? A youth group meeting? Try again. How about an introduction to philosophy class? How about a philosophy course in which I, the teacher, was probably the only Christian in the entire class? Yet the God question was the one the students wanted to discuss.

Actually, the course I was teaching had just concluded. For five months we had addressed the key questions of philosophy: What is real? What can we know? What is right and wrong? Does God exist? Thirty minutes earlier I had collected all the final test papers and then invited the students across the street to Al's Café. It was my reward for their hard effort in the course. Free chocolate malts at Al's, which serves the best shakes in the world!

I thought that after a long course and a hard final exam, the last thing the students would want to talk about was more of the same. But I was wrong—and pleasantly surprised. The first question asked after the malts were served was the God question. In fact, it was the only question they wanted to talk about. And we went on for nearly an hour!

The God Question

"Do you believe in God—and why?" Have you ever thought about this question? How would you answer it? Since you are reading this book, I imagine you have thought about it and maybe have even asked others the same question. I want to tell you how I answered it while drinking chocolate malts with my philosophy class. Of course, this question will lead to other questions: Who is God? What is God like? Can we really know God? Can we be like God? We will look at those issues as well.

Belief in God Is Universal

I believe in God. In fact, for as long as I can remember, I have believed in God. When my parents taught me to pray when I was very young, God was the one to whom I said my simple prayers. As I grew up, I believed that God loved me, though he was angry when I did wrong but happy when I did the right things. I tried to please God by living a good life and staying out of trouble—not always easy for a teenager! An interesting thing was that all my friends also believed in God like I did. Even now, as an adult, I'm amazed that just about everyone I meet—children, teens in high school, college students, working people, senior citizens, Americans, Europeans, Africans, Asians, men and women, rich people and poor, educated and simple people, Christians, Jews, Muslims, Hindus—believes in God. In other words, belief in God is universal.

So, how can we explain this phenomenon? There are actually five evidences that lead us to believe in God's existence.

Human Beings Have an Innate Sense of God

People everywhere simply have a sense that God exists. This universal belief is called an *innate sense of God*. If we think of people as computers, then we could say that all of us have all been hardwired with an idea of God. We are born with this sense, everyone has it, and try as we might, we can never get rid of it. What about atheists, people who claim that they don't believe in God? There's an old saying: "There are no atheists in foxholes." (Foxholes are underground areas that soldiers dig out when they come under attack from gunfire and bombs during a war.) In moments of grave danger, when peoples' lives are at great risk, they turn for help to God to save them from death. Those times may come during a serious illness or a near-fatal automobile accident. Whatever the circumstances, it is in those moments on the edge between life and death that our innate sense of God comes out—even in people who claim there is no God. Even they sense it then.

This innate sense of God can account for another phenomenon we see everywhere around us: people are religious. Now I'm not just talking about Christians going to church or Jews going to the synagogue, though that's certainly part of it. Throughout the world Muslims go to the mosque and observe special holy days like Ramadan; Buddhists practice the art of self-denial in their attempt to reach nirvana; people involved in the New Age movement try to stir up the God spark that is within them; even pagans worship the trees, rivers, and winds. Certainly many of these practices are far away from Christianity and its worship of God through Jesus Christ, but they do witness to the fact that people are religious at heart. And this again points out that people have an innate sense of God. People believe in God because he planted that belief in their hearts.

The Bible takes note of this. In fact, it is the reality that the apostle Paul addressed when he spoke with the philosophers of Athens: "Men of Athens! I see that you are extremely religious in every respect. For as I was passing through and observing the objects of your worship, I even found an altar on which was inscribed:

| TO AN UNKNOWN GOD |

Therefore, what you worship in ignorance, this I proclaim to you" (Acts 17:22–23).

So strong was the sense of God among these people that they engaged in the worship of idols—statues carved out of wood or cut from stone. To make sure they had not overlooked anyone in their religious devotion, these philosophers also built an altar to the true God—even though they knew nothing about him other than the belief that he existed. Paul explained to them that God was the one who created everything—the heavens, the earth, and the nations of the world. He then added, "so that they might seek God, and perhaps they might reach out and find Him, though He is not far from each one of us. For in Him we live and move and exist, as even some of your own poets have said, 'For we are also His offspring'" (Acts 17:27–28). Paul confirmed that the philosophers' basic instinct to worship God was exactly the way God had designed them. All people believe in God because God himself placed that sense within them.

God Reveals Himself through Creation

A second reason why people believe in God is his *revelation in creation*. A song entitled "Evidence of God" explains it this way:

I believe that William Shakespeare lived
Though we never met
'Cause when I was seventeen
I read *Romeo and Juliet*
And I believe there was a man
Whose name was Michelangelo
'Cause he left his mark
In a chapel in the heart of Rome

CHORUS:
Every mountain, every valley
Your creation it surrounds me
Every breath I breathe
Every heartbeat
Every sunrise that you give to me
These and so much more
Tell a story we cannot ignore
The evidence of God

As a potter shapes his clay
He leaves evidence
And our Father does the same
His creation is evidence
That's how we can believe in a God we cannot see
    or hear or touch
If we would open our eyes
We would see his work
It's all around us[1]

God leaves clear signs of his existence by the things he has made. His creation is evidence that God exists. The Bible tells us that this revelation in creation is a key for everyone to believe in God. The creation has the ability to communicate this message to everyone in the world without using words:

The heavens tell of the glory of God.

The skies display his marvelous craftsmanship.

Day after day they continue to speak;

night after night they make him known.

They speak without a sound or a word;

their voice is silent in the skies;

yet their message has gone out to all the earth,

and their words to all the world. (Psalm 19:1–4 NLT)

Paul also affirms the importance of creation's evidence for God's existence: "For God's wrath is revealed from heaven against all god-lessness and unrighteousness of people who by their unrighteous-ness suppress the truth, since what can be known about God is evi-dent among them, because God has shown it to them. From the creation of the world His invisible attributes, that is, His eternal power and divine nature, have been clearly seen, being understood through what He has made. As a result, people are without excuse" (Romans 1:18–20).

What can we learn about God from his revelation in creation? One thing we know is that God exists. The sun, moon, and stars; plants and animals; human beings; and whatever else exists did not make themselves. Instead, the entire creation is a marvelous craftsmanship brought into existence by God the Creator. The creation witnesses to the reality of the Creator. Second, we know something about what this Creator is like—the character of God. When we think about towering mountains, vast oceans, colorful fish and birds, brilliant sunsets, powerful winds, capa-ble doctors and creative artists, what do we learn about the God who created these things? We can certainly understand that he is an all-powerful, creative, beauty-loving, wise, skillful Creator. This revelation is intended to produce a certain effect on us as we view the creation. It should lead us to glorify this awesome

God—to worship him, praise him for his mighty works, and give him thanks!

Would that the story ends here—but it doesn't. Tragically, we respond to God's revelation of himself in creation in the wrong way. Rather than recognizing that God has created us, we push this truth away. We exchange the truth for a false idea and believe that lie. For example, some people today think that the things God created—the sun, mountains, fire, forests—are gods to be worshiped. Other people believe that the world and all that is in it has evolved over the course of time to become what it is today and that God has had little or nothing to do with this evolutionary process. Some go so far as to believe that aliens from another planet came to earth to create it. For example, the movie *Mission to Mars* pictures a Martian sending DNA (the building blocks of all life) on board a spaceship to earth, and from this DNA the first life-forms started and developed into plants, animals, and even human beings.

Paul has some harsh words for those of us who refuse to acknowledge God's role in creation: "For though they knew God, they did not glorify Him as God or show gratitude. Instead, their thinking became nonsense, and their senseless minds were darkened. Claiming to be wise, they became fools" (Romans 1:21–22).

Though we clearly see the revelation of God in creation, we respond to it in the wrong way. This spells doom for all of us. Indeed, Paul describes us as people "without excuse" (Romans 1:20) because we misread and misuse the evidence. That which God intended to help us believe in his existence and enable us to know something about his character will one day be evidence used against us. For when we come face-to-face with God himself, and he questions why we did not give him honor, no one will ever be able to say, "But I didn't know you exist!" God has left far too much evidence of himself in creation for that excuse to ever hold up.

God Reveals Himself through Providence

A third way that points people to belief in God is his *revelation in providence*—his care for the world. Have you ever considered that the very fact that you have food to eat every day is a witness to God and his goodness?

The Bible speaks about living in a world that runs its course under the caring direction of God. During one of the first missionary journeys ever, Paul and Barnabas came to a town named Lystra. After healing a lame man, they were mobbed by the crowd—the farmers thought the miracle-working apostles were gods. Paul and Barnabas seized this occasion to explain the true God: "Men! Why are you doing these things? We are men also, with the same nature as you, and we are proclaiming good news to you, that you should turn from these worthless things to the living God, 'who made the heaven, the earth, the sea, and everything in them.' In past generations He allowed all the nations to go their own way, although He did not leave Himself without a witness, since He did good: giving you rain from heaven and fruitful seasons, and satisfying your hearts with food and happiness" (Acts 14:15–17).

There has always been a witness to the existence of God. These reminders are his care in providing the essentials for people to live and be happy. The fact that we have seasons, rain, crops of wheat and corn, and food to eat point out important characteristics of God: he is a good, caring Father who provides for his children while ruling the world. Again, this revelation is intended to produce a certain effect on us as we consider God's providence in our lives. It should lead us to glorify this good God—to worship him, praise him for his care, and give him thanks. A simple prayer of thanks before we eat, or acknowledging God with the credit for something we have accomplished—these are the right ways to respond to this revelation of God.

Once again, however, our actual response to God's providence is off target. Rather than recognizing that it is God who watches out for us and provides for our needs, we give the credit to someone or something else. I'm amazed at news stories in which people who have barely avoided tornadoes or hurricanes say, "I was just at the right place at the right time!" They give the credit for escaping with their lives to chance. Or what about the people who come out of head-on car crashes with barely a scratch? "I sure was lucky today!" is their reaction. They give the credit to fate, not to God. Of course, you've heard of the "self-made" man or "self-made" woman. Who gets the credit for their accomplishments? *They* have worked hard, *they* have sacrificed, *they* have made themselves what they are today—and God is out of the picture. Remember Paul's strong words for those who fail to give God the credit he deserves: "Turn from these worthless things to the living God."

Our Consciences Point to God's Existence

A fourth reason why people believe in God is the *human conscience*. All people have a built-in moral compass, a sense of right and wrong, and this bears witness to God. Paul describes this when he discusses the difference between the Jews, who have the written law of God telling them right and wrong, and the Gentiles (everyone who is not Jewish). The Gentiles do not have the written law, but this doesn't put them at a disadvantage because a sense of right and wrong is built into every person: "All those who sinned without the law will also perish without the law, and all those who sinned under the law will be judged by the law. For the hearers of the law are not righteous before God, but the doers of the law will be declared righteous. So, when Gentiles, who do not have the law, instinctively do what the law demands, they are a law to themselves even though they do not have the law. They show that the work of the law is written on their hearts. Their consciences testify in support of this, and their competing thoughts either accuse or excuse them" (Romans 2:12–15).

Even Gentiles, who do not have the written law of right and wrong, instinctively know the difference between right and wrong because of their consciences. People everywhere and at all times know that killing another person is wrong and that telling lies is not right. They carry this moral sense in their hearts.

How does this instinctive knowledge help people believe in God? Well, where does this universal sense of right and wrong come from? It doesn't just come from being raised in a certain family, because this moral compass goes beyond family lines. It doesn't just arise from living in a certain country, because this sense of right and wrong crosses national boundaries. It doesn't just develop from living at a certain time in history, because this standard was the same centuries ago. Rather, it comes from being human beings to whom God has given a heart that knows right and wrong. In addition, this human conscience tells us something important about God: he is the one who determines what is right and wrong, and he expects people to do right and to avoid evil. Indeed, there is a universal sense that when we die, what we have done during our lives will be judged. This points out that God is a judge, and it encourages people to live the way he expects them to live.

So what do people do with this moral compass of right and wrong that points them to God? Paul holds out some hope for people when he notes that "their consciences testify in support of this, and their competing thoughts either accuse or excuse them." Perhaps you have felt peer pressure to do drugs, engage in sexual immorality, or participate in some crime, yet you refused to do so. If so, then you know the sense of confirmation that comes with doing the right thing. Your own heart applauds your action! But we all have experienced the opposite reality as well. The betrayal of a friend, the cutting remark to hurt others to make ourselves look better, even the blatant disobedience just for the sake of rebelling— these wrong actions are accompanied by a sense of guilt, shame, and embarrassment (even if no one else saw or knows about what we've done). This at least is the feeling at the start of the cycle of doing wrong. After awhile, the shame fades and people push away the guilt. There may even be a thrill at doing evil that replaces the embarrassment. Soon, people become so callused to doing wrong that it becomes second nature—it becomes easy to make the wrong choice over and over again. Yet even among those who have reached the point of being comfortable with doing wrong, I still find that they hate the hypocrisy of their own lives. Even though their moral compass has almost ceased working, they still hold on to some things they consider to be the right things to do. But they find that they can't even achieve those minimum hopes. Paul's words echo loudly in their case: "Their consciences . . . either accuse or excuse them."

Our human conscience was designed to give us a steady pointer to belief in God. But hope for this crumbles. We learn to free ourselves from the shame we sense—and should sense—when doing wrong. We dismiss our guilty feelings as unreasonable. We lower our standards, thinking this will make us feel good about not living up to the high expectations we once held for ourselves. But we still have a gnawing sense that things are not right—the prick of our conscience accuses us of violating the moral law of God. We try to reason it away by telling ourselves that our moral sense is just the product of our family upbringing or our society, but not from God. And since we are bigger than our family and bigger than our society, we can do as we please. We go into a terrible downward spiral when we try to rid ourselves of our God-consciousness. We shake our fist in anger at God: "You cannot and will not determine right and wrong for me! You cannot and will not hold me accountable for doing right and avoiding wrong! You cannot and will not be the judge of my conduct, now or later!" Yet despite all our protesting, our heart of hearts knows better—because God has built our conscience into it.

Now the first four reasons for belief in God that I've discussed are called *general revelation* because they are ways pointing to God that are true for *all* people at *all* times and in *all* places. Everyone everywhere has an innate sense of God; everyone everywhere sees God's revelation in creation; everyone everywhere experiences God's revelation in providence; and everyone everywhere possesses a conscience. No wonder belief in God is so common and widespread!

The Bible Specifically Reveals God

A fifth and final way that directs people to belief in God is a bit different and makes up another category of reasons why people believe in God. This is called *special revelation* because it is directed only to *certain* people at *certain* times and in *certain* places. The *Bible* is God's special revelation. It tells people of his existence and presents what he is like. The Bible does not, however, try to prove God's existence. It takes that fact for granted. Notice how the Bible begins: "In the beginning God created the heavens and the earth" (Genesis 1:1). Here's the great assumption of the Bible: God exists.

The Bible then goes on to relate—through stories, poetry, visions of the future, gospels, letters, and so forth—what God is like. What can we learn about God from the Bible? We can learn that God is full of love, good to all people, powerful in every way, angered by sin, pleased by faith and obedience, merciful and forgiving, worthy of our worship, and much more. In fact, if we take our list of what we can learn about God from his general revelation and compare it with our list of what we can know from his special revelation in the Bible, the two lists are nearly identical! The Bible confirms what we can know of God from creation, providence, and so forth. There is no conflict from the two revelations. The Bible does add some things we can't know about God from general revelation—for example, that he is three persons: Father, Son and Holy Spirit. The Bible is a more complete way of knowing God.

This is a key reason why you and I as followers of Jesus Christ have been given the task of communicating the Bible to others. It is the most complete revelation we possess that points people to belief in God. We have also seen how each of the other revelations fails in one way or another. Remember, this failure is not due to the revelations themselves. The innate sense of God still runs strong in people; the revelation in creation is wonderfully displayed for all to see; the revelation in providence is experienced daily by anyone who has food to eat; and the human conscience continues to denounce doing wrong and to confirm doing right. The data input is not the problem—the problem lies with how we process the data we have. Human nature is such that we consistently read the data and draw the wrong conclusions: people worship something or someone other than God; they trace their origin to evolution or aliens instead of God; they acknowledge luck or fate for the good fortune they experience instead of recognizing God; and they push away the moral law of God and set their own standards in its place. That is why people desperately need a sure word from God that can overcome human error and put them on the right track back to God. The Bible is God's Word that we share with them to do just that.

As my philosophy students and I sat around the table at Al's Café drinking our chocolate malts and discussing the God question, I knew I had to introduce the class to the Word of God if I wanted them to have the clearest and most sure revelation of God. As I talked about the Bible, I challenged them to read it as a witness that would enable them to believe in God. What excites me is that this story repeats itself every time you and I share the Word with others. And just think: every day, millions of Christians around the world do this. To be part of a movement like this—well, there can't be anything better!

 A thought: Why don't you ask some of your friends the question my philosophy class asked me as we drank chocolate malts: "Do you believe in God—and why?" See which of the five reasons they give you. And don't forget to ask yourself that same question! Remember: Many people think this question is one of the most important questions that can be asked, so think carefully about it.

Believing and Knowing

CHAPTER 2

My wife and I used to be staff members of Campus Crusade for Christ. Our first ministry was working with college students at the University of Notre Dame. One effective method of engaging ND students in conversation was using a survey with a series of questions about God and other spiritual topics. At the top of the list was the question we just discussed: "Do you believe in God?" Every student we interviewed at Notre Dame answered yes to that first question. As we worked our way through the survey, however, it often became clear that the students' belief in God had little or no impact on their lives. Some thought about God occasionally, and a few even prayed somewhat regularly. Other than that, belief in God had little relevance for their lives as students. This became especially evident when we came to the last question on the survey: "If you could know God personally, would you be interested?" Most students had a puzzled look on their faces and wondered, "What does it mean to know God personally?"

Believing vs. Knowing

Would you agree there is a huge difference between believing and knowing? Sure, both are actions we commonly engage in, and both require us to focus on something or someone outside of ourselves. But there seems to be a world of difference between them. Students from Notre Dame can believe in God, but that belief can exert little influence on how they live. The philosophers from Athens or the farmers from Lystra can believe in God, but they honor God wrongly by worshiping idols—statues of birds, animals, and people. "Self-made" people can believe in God, but they fail to acknowledge that God is the one who has given them their abilities. But people who know God—there's something more to it, isn't there? *Knowing* God presents us with the idea of having a personal relationship with God, and that goes deeper and is more intense than just believing in God. *Believing* in God gives us a picture of someone who checks off an intellectual box in his mind: *Yes, I am of the opinion that some divine being greater than me exists.* It begins and ends there. But *knowing* seems to demand trust, obedience, commitment, intimacy—a true and meaningful friendship. The truth is, knowing God—not just believing in him—is what we want. What's more, knowing him—not just believing in him—is what God wants for us as well.

Can We Know God?

Is a personal relationship with God possible? I once had a conversation with a friend who is an agnostic (someone who doesn't think—indeed, even doubts—that God can be known). He informed me, "Even if God could be known, I hope that he doesn't bother about me because he has far more important things to do—like keeping the universe in existence and running right!" Put that way, I guess my friend had a point. Doesn't it seem rather presumptuous on our part to hope that we can know God? After all, we are rather insignificant creatures when you consider the vast numbers of plants and animals and stars and galaxies that God has to worry about. Perhaps our hope is greatly misplaced. How can we tiny, finite (or limited) beings ever hope to know the perfect, infinite (or unlimited) God? It does sound rather preposterous!

In a way, my friend is right. The perfect, infinite God who made the universe and rules over it is *incomprehensible*—he cannot be known, at least not fully. Try as we might for as long as we can, we limited human beings can never know everything about God. In fact, we can never *fully* know even one thing about God. We can never completely know his love, understand his wisdom, or be able to figure out his ways. He is incomprehensible—we can never fully grasp God.

Don't let this discourage you, however, because the Bible affirms that we can know God. Not totally, of course, because he is incomprehensible. But he is *knowable*. Listen to what the prophet Jeremiah says about the most important thing in the world, something so awesome that God himself tells us to boast about it: "This is what the LORD says: 'Let not the wise man gloat in his wisdom, or the mighty man in his might, or the rich man in his riches. Let them boast in this alone: that they truly know me and understand that I am the LORD who is just and righteous, whose love is unfailing, and that I delight in these things. I, the LORD, have spoken!'" (Jeremiah 9:23–24 NLT).

The greatest possible claim to fame is not that we come from a wealthy family so that we are financially set for life, or that we have set some kind of high school record in swimming, cross-country running, or scoring in basketball. It isn't being the homecoming queen or the star football player. It's not about performing a solo in the choir, being first-chair violin, or playing music for Jesus in an alternative band. It doesn't come from wearing the latest name-brand clothes, or even from wearing the most absurd clothes. It's not about being the smartest or the sexiest or the smoothest. The greatest possible claim to fame is that we know God.

If this is the case, then knowing God must be what life is all about. Jesus himself said as much when he gave this definition of eternal life in one of his prayers to the Father: "This is eternal life— to know you, the only true God, and Jesus Christ, the one you sent to earth" (John 17:3; author's translation). Though many may think of eternal life as a reality that begins at death—life that extends beyond our earthly existence—it is instead a present possession of Christians. It consists of knowing God—enjoying a personal relationship with him and his Son, Jesus Christ. The Bible makes it clear that knowing God is not only possible, it is the very essence of life itself. Though we cannot know God completely, nor even any one thing about God totally, we can know God through a personal relationship with him and his Son.

 Your turn: Do you think there is a difference between believing in God and knowing God? What would you say the major difference is? As you evaluate your own life, would you say that you believe in God or know God? What would it take for you to move from believing in God to knowing God? Perhaps you know someone who believes in God, but you want to help your friend move on to knowing God. What do you think you could share with that friend to help in this process?

The Mystery of God's Identity

CHAPTER 3

"Nora, you just need to believe in God!"

"But who is God, and what is he like?"

Even as a kid, my wife, Nora, was very inquisitive. So when people encouraged her to believe in God, she was always ready with a question about the identity of this God. Whether it was a family member or one of her friends, Nora posed the question and waited for the response. One of her greatest frustrations was not receiving a convincing answer. As she grew older, the replies became more sophisticated, but she still never received an answer that persuaded her. For example:

- At age 5: "God is an old man with a long white beard who sits on a throne in heaven."
- At age 12: "God is love. God is goodness. God is your conscience."
- At age 17: "God is the one who is responsible for the creation we see."

By the time she finished high school, Nora began to wonder if God could ever be known. As she packed her bags and went off to college, she took with her the same unanswered question—the mystery of God's identity: "But who is God, and what is he like?"

Defining God

By the time people reach high school, they realize the importance of being able to write good definitions. A good definition helps identify a problem, clarify an issue, or avoid misunderstanding. In some cases, writing a good definition is fairly easy, especially when it comes to concrete things like Tiger Woods and the SAT exam. In other cases, coming up with a good definition is challenging, especially when dealing with abstract matters such as freedom, beauty, and love.

Perhaps that was the problem with Nora's family and friends when she asked them about the identity of God. Perhaps the task of "defining" God is just so complex that any attempt is bound to fail. But if we affirm that we believe in God and even claim to know him, doesn't that personal relationship with God imply that we know who he is and what he is like? Shouldn't we be able to define God—to unravel the mystery of his identity?

What Is God Like?

Knowing that the task is a difficult one, some people still make attempts at defining God. They would be the first to recognize that any definition will limit God, who—by definition!—can't be limited. By noting this, we can see that any definition of God will necessarily play a limited role. But as long as we keep this in mind, we should be helped by the attempt. Here is one definition from a long time ago: "God is a Spirit. He is infinite, eternal and unchangeable in his being, wisdom, power, holiness, justice, goodness and truth."[1]

If we take a close look at this definition, we see that it defines God by listing his attributes, the characteristics that make God what he is. Just as our friends would "define" us by naming their favorite things about us—we are friendly, kind, honest, loyal, helpful, understanding, funny—so we "define" God by naming his traits or attributes. He is wise, powerful, pure, right, good, and true. Being infinite, God possesses these attributes without any limits: he is completely wise, powerful in every way, totally pure, right in all his actions, perfectly good, and true at all times. Being eternal, there has never been a beginning to God and his attributes, and he never will be an end. Also, God never changes. He cannot learn something new so as to become more intelligent and wiser, and he cannot exercise more to gain strength so as to be more powerful.

Because he never does wrong, he cannot stop sinning to purify himself; and since he always does what is right, he can't become a better ruler of the universe. He can never increase in goodness so as to be more loving, kind, gracious, and merciful. Because he cannot lie and he cannot break his promises, he cannot become more truthful and faithful. In other words, we should never expect to see a new and improved God!

How Do We Know What God Is Like?

If we are going to engage in listing the characteristics of God, what will be the source for our knowledge of his attributes? We have two sources for that information: general revelation and the Bible.

General Revelation. An interesting experiment would be to go to a shopping mall and find some people who are taking a break from buying stuff or who are just hanging around. If we asked them the question Nora posed—"Who is God, and what is he like?"—I think we would be amazed to find their list to be much like the definition given above. When people think about God, everyone agrees that he is present everywhere, he is powerful in all ways, and he knows everything. Everyone says that God is good, he takes care of the world, and he loves everyone. Everyone thinks that God is perfect, holy, and right in everything he does. In other words, everyone can list the "great-making properties" of God. This brings us back to general revelation. From an innate sense of God, from his revelation in creation and providence, and from their conscience, people know something of what God is like. We can know God's attributes through general revelation. That is one source for us to know the "great-making properties" of God.

The Bible. As we already said in chapter 1, the Bible is a more complete revelation of God than general revelation. As we discuss who God is and what he is like, the best source for our understanding of his characteristics will be the Bible. It not only confirms what we know from general revelation, it also reveals additional important information that helps us know him better.

God's Attributes

As we discover who God is by identifying his characteristics, we see that his nature is actually made up of two types of attributes: his *incommunicable attributes* and his *communicable attributes*.

On the one hand, *incommunicable attributes* are those that God alone possesses. We find nothing quite like the incommunicable attributes of God in us—they are not reflected in our lives. For example, God is independent. He does not depend on anyone or anything for his existence. This is unlike us because we completely depend both on God and our parents for our existence. Also, God is immutable; he never changes. Contrast that with how we are constantly changing—physically, in our knowledge and abilities, in our relationships, and so forth.

The *communicable attributes,* on the other hand, are those that we share with God—or, better, that he shares with us. God shares his nature with us so that some of his attributes actually appear in our lives. God is love, isn't he? And we are able to love, aren't we? So the love of God is reflected in us when we love, even if our love is very limited, quite imperfect, and not always expressed in the right way. God is truthful, isn't he? And we can tell the truth, can't we? So the truthfulness of God is reflected in us when we tell the truth, even when we struggle to do so, sometimes preferring to stretch the truth or even lie. God is faithful, isn't he? And we are faithful at times, aren't we? So the faithfulness of God is reflected in us when we honor our commitments and fulfill promises we have made, even if we promise things we can't deliver or commit to things we should avoid. And so it goes. We are like God in many ways, and those characteristics we share with him are his communicable attributes.

At the beginning of this chapter, Nora just wanted a clear and convincing answer to her question: "Who is God, and what is he like?" In the next several chapters I will attempt to answer her question by searching out what the Bible has to say about both the incommunicable and communicable attributes of God.

 Ask some people at school what they think God is like. Or take a friend to the mall and ask some shoppers how they would describe God. Make a list of these "great-making properties" of God. Then ask yourself the question that Nora asked: "Who is God, and what is he like?" How does your answer compare with the list of God's attributes that other people gave? Do you see any major differences? Do you find qualities that other people listed that you don't think are true of God? Did you come up with characteristics that other people didn't? How do you explain the differences between your idea of God and the views of others? Do you think it may have something to do with different sources for knowledge about God that you and they used?

God's
Complete Uniqueness

My wife and I spent a relaxing few days in Victoria, British Columbia, Canada. For our accommodations, we found a peaceful bed and breakfast in an out-of-the-way place. It was run by a friendly couple, and one morning they invited us to eat with them. In the course of our conversation we discovered that they are followers of Feng Shui, an Eastern religion that encourages people to seek balance in the many activities of life and to find peace with oneself and with others. Feng Shui also encourages people to view God any way they please. Those from a Christian background can believe in God in that way, and those who conceive of God according to Hinduism, Islam, Buddhism, or any other religion are encouraged to believe in God in those ways as well.

We pressed this couple about their beliefs about God. They said they prefer to view God as compassionate and loving— never judging and condemning anyone for doing evil. Because this couple was very tolerant and nonjudgmental, their view of God reflected their ideals. They emphasized that all followers of Feng Shui can imagine God any way they like, and they were simply sharing their own personal beliefs about him. Though they might have felt uncomfortable about our belief that God is not only compassionate and full of love but also perfectly holy so as to act against sin, they would not disagree with us about our belief.

As we walked away following our interesting conversation with this couple, we were struck by one fact: the God whom we Christians know and worship is completely different from the way other religions view their supreme beings. Their "gods" are little more than human ideals, similar in many ways to the people who believe in them.

There Are None Like God

God is totally unique. Even to say this falls far short of the reality of God's uniqueness; he is so completely "other" that he exists in a class all by himself. Imagine taking an inventory of everything that exists in the universe. On the one hand, into one category we would list human beings, angels, animals, plants, rocks, bodies of water, the atmosphere, galaxies and stars, and so forth. On the other hand, we would have another category all by itself—and the only member who would be listed in it is God. This means that God is completely different from all other supreme beings that claim the title "god." This also means that God is totally different from us human beings. But how is God unique and completely set apart from us?

How Is God Unique?

God's uniqueness is emphasized by certain attributes that put him into a category all by himself. Called *incommunicable attributes,* they are ones that God alone possesses. They are not in us— in fact, they are not even reflected in our lives. God is unique because he is completely independent (or self-sufficient), never changing, eternal, and present everywhere.

God Is Independent

God is unique because he is completely *independent.* He does not depend on anyone or anything for his existence. Everything else that exists—you and me included—is dependent or a contingent creature. First and foremost, we are contingent on God's will and plan to create us. Secondly, we depend on parents to provide the biological building blocks—sperm, egg, DNA—for our existence. In fact, it could have been the case that we never existed. What if God had not willed for us to be part of his plan? What if our parents had not gotten together to produce us? Because we are contingent creatures, our existence is dependent on other people and other events.

This is not so with God. As completely self-sufficient, he does not depend on anyone or anything for his existence. The apostle Paul emphasizes this attribute of God: "The God who made the world and everything in it—He is Lord of heaven and earth and does not live in shrines made by hands. Neither is He served by human hands, as though He needed anything, since He Himself gives everyone life and breath and all things" (Acts 17:24–25).

Proof that God is independent—not a creature in need of anyone or anything else—is the fact that he is the Creator of the world and everything that exists. Because he has life in himself, he is able to give life to everything else. This is the great distinction between Creator and creature: Our God, the Creator, is independent, self-sufficient. We as his creatures are contingent, dependent on him and others for our existence.

As Paul noted, God's independence means that *he does not need us*. Not only this, but God *could not* need us for anything. How could our completely self-sufficient God need anything at all? He doesn't need us to love him because love has always existed between the Father, the Son, and the Holy Spirit. He couldn't need us because of loneliness, for the same reason: the Father, the Son, and the Holy Spirit have always enjoyed personal relationships with each other. (I'll talk more about this in later chapters.) God doesn't and couldn't need us to fill up something lacking in him because he is complete in himself.

So why did God create us? I will give a positive answer to this question in the next chapter, but now I want to give a negative answer to it based on the fact of God's independence. *He did not create us because he needs us.* That's my negative answer. Because he is completely self-sufficient, God did not create us because he *needs* us to love him, serve him, relate to him, or anything else like that. But—and this is a very important qualification—because our independent, all-sufficient God did create us, our existence must have incredible significance! The very fact that we exist as people created by God must mean that we are very special creatures. We are significant because God created us and made us significant. When we trust God, when we read his Word and obey him, when we understand his will and follow him, when we engage in worshiping God—when we do anything that's in harmony with God's plan—we please him. Conversely, when we have little faith, when we disobey, when we choose our own path rather than his way, when we sin—when we do anything that's against God's will—we displease him. Though God does not need anything—including you and me—we can still please him or displease him. This is due to the fact that he created us with great significance. Our life is marked by dignity because our all-sufficient God made us in such a way that we are very significant to him.

PAUSE TIME— Pause button: Take a few moments to reflect on God's attribute of independence. You may want to write your thoughts down. How does it make you feel to know that God is completely self-sufficient and therefore does not and could not need us? What great dignity do you enjoy because God created you? How significant are you to God? As I reflect on this, God's personal decision that I should exist assures me that I am not just a statistic among the six-billion-plus people in the world today. If I were merely a number among that mass of people, who would really care who I am and what I do? Who would even care if I live or die? God's independence means I am very significant to him—he cares!

God Never Changes

God is also unique because he never changes. The *immutability* of God means that God does not and cannot change. This is in great contrast with everything else that exists, as this prayer to God notes:

In the beginning you laid the foundations of the earth,
and the heavens are the work of your hands.
They will perish, but you remain;
they will all wear out like a garment.
Like clothing you will change them
and they will be discarded.
But you remain the same,
and your years will never end. (Psalm 102:25–27)

Here again is the great distinction between Creator and creation: God does not change, but the heavens, the earth, and all of creation do. God will never get worse, and he can never get better. He himself says, "I the LORD do not change" (Malachi 3:6).

We see God's immutability in four areas: God is unchanging as a *person*. He has always existed and will always exist as the Father, the Son, and the Holy Spirit. The Trinity is eternal and never changes. God is also unchanging in his attributes or *perfections*. He is always loving, perfectly just, constantly faithful, eternally true, forever good, and so forth. God is unchanging with respect to his *plans*. The following psalm notes a contrast between our plans and God's plans:

The LORD foils the plans of the nations;
he thwarts the purposes of the peoples.
But the plans of the LORD stand firm forever,
the purposes of his heart through all generations.
(Psalm 33:10–11)

This means that whatever God has planned to do—and he constructed his plan before he brought the universe into existence—will certainly come about. As Paul affirms, "In Him we were also made His inheritance, predestined according to the purpose of the One who works out everything in agreement with the decision of His will" (Ephesians 1:11). This includes his plan for you and me. His will for us is absolutely perfect, his good purpose will never change, and his plan will be accomplished in and through our lives. God will never be like a friend who makes plans to do something with us and then backs out.

Finally, God is unchanging in regard to his *promises:*
"God is not a man, that he should lie,
    nor a son of man, that he should change his mind.
Does he speak and then not act?
    Does he promise and not fulfill?" (Numbers 23:19)

The answer to these questions is "No. Of course not!" God does not commit himself to something and then go back on his promise. He will never be like a friend who promises to return a borrowed CD but then keeps it. God cannot say that he will do something—like "I will give you eternal life"—and then announce, "Just kidding!" He does not lie, and he cannot change his mind because he is unchanging in his promises.

All this talk about God's unchangeableness should not lead us to conclude that God is somehow like an unfeeling, static robot who is unaffected by the people and events of this world. God feels emotions—joy, grief, anger, pleasure, jealousy, love, wrath, and delight—and he acts and feels differently in different situations. When we do the right thing, the pleasure that God feels is more intense and more satisfying than the greatest joy we could ever imagine. On the other hand, when we displease him, the disgust that God senses is deeper and more upsetting than any heartbreak we could ever experience. We should never allow our idea of the immutability of God to detract from the truth that he relates to us in a very personal way. As he remains constantly stable in relation to his person, perfections, plans, and promises, God intimately relates to us and responds to our different situations in different ways.

 A disturbing thought: What would life be like if God could change? What would it be like if God himself changed? Or if one or more of his attributes changed? How would you be affected if God's plans could change? What would be the result if God's promises could change?

God Is Eternal

Another attribute that makes God unique is the fact that he is *eternal*. This means that God is infinite with respect to time. The prophet Isaiah described God as "he who lives forever" (Isaiah 57:15). Psalm 90 proclaims:

Before the mountains were born
 or you brought forth the earth and the world,
from everlasting to everlasting you are God. (v. 2)

God has always existed, he exists right now, and he will always exist. God never came into existence; there never was a time in the past in which he did not exist. God will never go out of existence; there never will be a time in the future in which he will not exist. His existence has neither beginning nor end.

Though God is eternal, he is able to relate to time and act in time. God does certain things *before* he does others. For example, God "chose us in [Christ], before the foundation of the world, to be holy and blameless in His sight" (Ephesians 1:4). God's plan to enter into a personal relationship with us through his Son was designed before he created the universe. Also, God does some things *after* he does others. For example, Paul describes a series of future events that will occur in an ordered sequence: "For just as in Adam all die, so also in Christ all will be made alive. But each in his own order: Christ, the firstfruits; afterward, at His coming, the people of Christ. Then comes the end, when He hands over the kingdom to God the Father, when He abolishes all rule and all authority and power" (1 Corinthians 15:22–24).

First comes the resurrection of Christ, *then* our resurrection, *then* the end. This shows that God is able to relate to time and act in time, doing some things before he does others and doing some things after he does others.

Yet, God enjoys a unique relationship to time as well. The psalmist explains that "a thousand years in [God's] sight are like a day that has just gone by" (Psalm 90:4), and Peter adds that "with the Lord one day is like a thousand years, and a thousand years like one day" (2 Peter 3:8). These verses indicate that God possesses a unique sense of time. His "memory" of past events is so vivid that he experiences them as if they just occurred. Thus, God knows the entire past—the history of the world since it was created—as if it had just taken place. God also knows each individual day—with its many events and different activities—with similar clarity because each day continues to be present in God's mind forever. God experiences everything—the past, the present, and the future—with equal vividness.

God Is Everywhere

God is unique because he is present everywhere. The *omnipresence* of God (*omni* means "all" or "everywhere") is his infinity with respect to space. A series of questions by God himself reveals that he is present everywhere in the universe:

"Am I only a God nearby,"
 declares the LORD,
"and not a God far away?
 Can anyone hide in secret places
so that I cannot see him?"
 declares the LORD.
"Do not I fill heaven and earth?"
 declares the LORD. (Jeremiah 23:23–24)

God is not only near us where we are located; he is also far away, filling the entire universe. When we hear this, we may tend to think about God as being really big—being

ABSOLUTELY HUGE!

But this is not the right way to imagine God's omnipresence. He cannot be contained in the space of the universe. Solomon, one of the kings of Israel, expressed this when he dedicated the temple to be a special location for God to dwell with his people: "But will God really dwell on earth? The heavens, even the highest heaven, cannot contain you. How much less this temple I have built!" (1 Kings 8:27). Though God may indeed be near us—even living in a temple constructed for his special presence—he is not confined to these locations. In fact, the entire universe cannot contain him. We should not imagine God as being "bigger" than the universe. Thinking this way limits him. God doesn't have spatial dimensions; he exists without height, depth, breadth, and width.

We should also not imagine God as being present with part of his being (his love, for example) in one place and present with another part of his being (his justice, for example) in another place. Again, this way of thinking pictures God as being composed of parts—like a model of elements and their bonds used in chemistry class. Rather, God is present everywhere with his whole being. The fullness of God and his love, justice, truthfulness, holiness, grace, and mercy exist everywhere.

Though he is present everywhere with his whole being, God is present in different ways in different places and at different times. God is present with *everything that he has created* to sustain it and keep his creation in existence. He is present with *all people everywhere* to provide the necessities of food and water that they need to live. This reminds them of his goodness and care for them. God is present graciously with *all those who don't yet know Christ* to unsettle them about their current life and to speak to them about his Son. He is present with *new believers* to help them reorient their lives from self-centeredness to God-centeredness. He is present joyfully with *growing Christians* to guide them, equip and use them for ministry, and give them his many good gifts. He is present sternly with *carnal Christians*—those who have turned their backs on Christ while wandering away from God—to discipline them and turn them around in the right direction. He is with *you and me* as we lie alone at night or drive down a deserted, lonely road—even if we don't think he is present. God's presence in all these instances reminds us that God is not a static, unmoving, and unfeeling being. Rather, he intimately relates to us by being present in different ways according to our different situations.

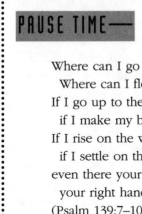

I want you to know and count on something: God's omnipresence is very important for you. David writes:

Where can I go from your Spirit?
Where can I flee from your presence?
If I go up to the heavens, you are there;
if I make my bed in the depths, you are there.
If I rise on the wings of the dawn,
if I settle on the far side of the sea,
even there your hand will guide me,
your right hand will hold me fast.
(Psalm 139:7–10)

Is there any place you can go where God is not present? Is there any situation in which you may find yourself that God is not with you? Is there any space so dark or ominous, so fearful or wretched, that God does not appear? Sometimes God may seem far off—indeed, you may fight and complain angrily against a "silent" God—but he is present with you. He is always ready to rescue you, comfort you as you cry and choke back your tears, turn you around, and guide you on the right path. You may think that you stray far from God, but only you have moved. God is right there with you, and he is with you all the way.

God Is Spirit

God is absolutely unique because he is independent, unchangeable, eternal, and present everywhere. These incommunicable attributes help us understand that God's being is unlike that of any other person or thing. Though we are made of matter—flesh, blood, and bones—God is not material. He does not have a physical body. Though the sun, power plants, and nuclear explosions produce energy, God is not energy. Though the forces of nature include wind, fire, and water, God is not some element of creation. Though we are able to think, remember, and imagine, God is not some process of thought. In other words, God is unlike anything else that exists.

So what is God like? When speaking with a woman at a well about the proper location for worship, Jesus himself said, "God is spirit" (John 4:24). By saying this Jesus means that God is not in one place or another so that people must go to one location or another in order to worship him. Rather, he exists in a completely different realm—a spiritual realm—that is completely unlike any other realm. God himself is spirit—his existence is totally unique and is more excellent than any other kind of existence. He is also invisible. Paul describes God as the one who "[dwells] in unapproachable light, whom none of mankind has seen or can see" (1 Timothy 6:16). While we live on earth, we cannot see God. That will change only when we go to heaven to be with him. The apostle John explains, "We will see Him as He is" (1 John 3:2).

No wonder the Bible has strong warnings against making idols or images of God. For example, the second commandment states: "You shall not make for yourself an idol in the form of anything in heaven above or on the earth beneath or in the waters below. You shall not bow down to them or worship them" (Exodus 20:4–5). Any such attempt would seriously compromise God because it would limit him by our human imagination. We would reduce God to something with which we are familiar. But God is different from anything and everything else that exists. We must wait until we actually meet God to see him as he truly is. Then, and only then, will we be captivated by the real vision of the true and absolutely unique God himself!

Seeing God in Prayer

How can we come "face-to-face" with God now? For example, how should we think about God when we pray? When my Feng Shui friends meditate, they try to empty their minds of all thoughts and simply feel peace and harmony. Of course this doesn't make sense if we have a personal relationship with God and talk with him directly in prayer. Rather, we should focus on God as he presents himself to us in his Word. He is our Father, so we should thankfully face him as the one who loves and protects us. He is our

Lord and King, so we should be ready with complete submission to trust and obey whatever he tells us. He is our forgiving Savior, so we should openly and honestly confess our sins with a sure expectation that he cleanses us.

We have already considered four of God's attributes, and we will soon see more. As we need something and pray, we can come "face-to-face" with God while meditating on those attributes that particularly apply to our situation. If we are confused and need direction to move ahead, we can approach him as our all-knowing and wise God. If we are in dire straits, we can cling to him as our compassionate, merciful God. If we are disturbed by unfairness and bigotry, we can rely on him as our righteous and just God. By facing God in prayer in this way, we avoid trying to picture God; instead, we focus our thoughts on who is he and what he does.

•••••••••••••••••••••

God is absolutely unique in his independence, immutability, eternity, and omnipresence. This means he is very different from us. In certain ways, however, God is very much like us—or, better, we are very much like God. What's more, this is part of his design for human beings. In the next chapter we will discuss what God had planned for us when he created us.

The Mirror Image of God

CHAPTER 5

What did you see when you looked at yourself in the mirror today?

I suppose the answer to this question depends on when you looked. If it was when you first woke up, I'm guessing there wasn't much to be pleased with. Because I went to bed last night with my hair wet, I woke up this morning with a 'do that stuck straight up in the air! Having not shaved for two days, the stubble on my face made me look quite unsightly. And not being a morning person, my first glance in the mirror revealed something closer to a zombie than a living human being!

The situation changes when we stand before the mirror after putting some time and effort into fixing up our appearance. For girls, makeup covers a multitude of imperfections and can magically transform a face. For us guys—well, we just naturally look good! Whatever the case, we spend part of each day in front of a mirror doing what we can to adjust our face and make it presentable to ourselves and others.

Have you ever stood in front of your mirror and thought about seeing something of God there? One of my favorite songs has a few lines that challenge us to do just that:

Then the morning comes and the mirror's another place
Where we wrestle face-to-face
With the image of deity.[1]

Human beings—you and I—are the image of deity. We have been created in the image of God; therefore, when we look at ourselves in the mirror, we get a glimpse of God himself. Sure, that image is very, very imperfect. Certainly what we see when we look in the mirror falls far short of God himself. Nonetheless here is a great truth: What we see in the mirror is a reflection of God himself because *he made us in his image.*

I hope you never look at yourself in the mirror the same way again.

Reflecting God's Image

I promised earlier that I would give a positive answer to the question, "Why did God create us?" Based on the reality of his independence, I first said that God did not create us because he needs us. That was my negative answer. Here is my positive answer: *God created us in his image so that we, like a mirror, would reflect him in the world in which we live.*

During his work of creation, God reserved a very special place for his creation of human beings. According to Genesis, God created the heavens and the earth, light, the sun and moon and stars, dry land and water, plants, fish, birds, land animals, and everything else in preparation for one more crowning effort—his creation of humanity. Everything that he created was leading up to that point. Before embarking on his final creative act, God deliberated among himself. In counsel together, the Father, the Son, and the Holy Spirit decided: "Let us make man in our image, in our likeness, and let them rule over the fish of the sea and the birds of the air, over the livestock, over all the earth, and over all the creatures that move along the ground" (Genesis 1:26). God purposed to create one more kind of being that would be more like himself than any other creature. He decided to create us—not fish, not birds, not animals, not even angels, but human beings. We would be the apex, the highlight, of his creation. And we, unlike any and all other created beings, would be made in his image.

Having completed this deliberation, God actualized what he purposed to do: "So God created man in his own image, in the image of God he created him; male and female he created them" (Genesis 1:27). Human beings are created in God's image. Just as an image—a photograph, a poster, a statue—reflects its original, so we are created to reflect God himself. As incredible as it may sound, we are a mirror that displays a visible image of our invisible Creator. As others see us, they catch a glimpse of what God himself is like.

In the past, Christians have attempted to identify the image of God as only part of our human nature. For example, some have thought that the image is our *rationality,* our ability to reason. Others have pointed to our *free will,* our ability to decide and to act for ourselves (and not according to instinct, as in the case of animals). Some have insisted that the image is our *potential for God,* our capacity to develop a relationship with God that is not enjoyed by any other created being. Still others have said that the image of God is our *function;* when we exercise our task of ruling over the earth and its creatures, then we are bearing God's image. All these ideas tend to reduce the image of God to one particular part or aspect of our humanness.

All of these proposals, however, miss a key point: We human beings are not made in a piecemeal way, like the pieces of a jigsaw puzzle that fit together to become a finished picture are. Rather, in our humanness, we are constructed holistically—with a wholeness and completeness that doesn't allow us to be divided into this part or that part. We as human beings in our entirety—not a part of us, not one particular ability or function—are created in the image of God. Each of us is the image of God.

Some would say that this is especially true of our soul and its characteristics of love, truthfulness, goodness, and so forth. But it is true of our body as well. God himself does not have a body, but he has created us as his image-bearers with a body so that we can do the kinds of things he does without a body. For example, God "sees" everything we do and all that goes on in the universe. He does his seeing without eyes, but he has given us eyes so that we can see as he does. God "hears" everything we say and all that is spoken in the world. He does his hearing without ears, but he has given us ears so that we can hear as he does. God "speaks"— indeed, he spoke and the universe was created, and he spoke and his Word was written down as our Bible. He does his speaking without a mouth, but he has given us a mouth so that we can speak as he does. God "acts" and "moves" in powerful ways—to rescue his people from Egypt by dividing the waters of the Red Sea, and to save us through the death and resurrection of Jesus Christ. He accomplishes his actions without arms, and he moves without legs; but he has given us arms and legs so that we can act and move as he does. Our body is essential to our creation in the image of God—it enables us to reflect him in very concrete ways.

There is one more important truth we learn from God's creation of us (and I'll return to this later on): As we read in Genesis 1:27, when God created *man* (note the singular noun) in his image, he created *them* (note the plural noun) male and female. God not only created us as unique individuals, he created us as social beings as well. We are designed to be closely related in a community composed of men and women. In one sense, whereas each of us is created in God's image, that image is most fully reflected as we live together in dynamic, loving relationships. While you and I, as individual image-bearers, can reflect God, it is together in relationship in a community that we most fully reflect God to the world in which we live.

If we think carefully about this, it really shouldn't surprise us. Before creating us, the Father, the Son, and the Holy Spirit had always loved each other in the community of the Trinity. They had always experienced dynamic, loving relationships. When God created us in his image, he desired that those same dynamic, loving relationships would be reflected in our human community. By creating us as men and women, God constructed humanity in such a way that we could be a mirror of the community of the Father, the Son, and the Holy Spirit.

God created us in his image so that we, like a mirror, would reflect him in the world in which we live. This is the positive reason why God, who did not need us because he is completely self-sufficient, created us. This reason provides us with the answer to one of the most important questions about life that could ever be asked: "Why do I exist?" "Does human existence have meaning?" "What is the purpose for my life?" We exist to reflect God in the world in which we live. Human existence has meaning because we are created with dignity and significance as the image-bearers of God. Our purpose is to imitate him. As we do, we give others a glimpse of what God himself is like. This is most clearly and convincingly accomplished as we build a community of men and women characterized by dynamic, loving relationships.

The Church: The Community of God's Image-Bearers

While reflecting God to the world is the purpose of all people—because everyone is created in God's image—it becomes especially true of us Christians. Through our relationship with God, we are helped to realize God's purpose for our lives. We not only have a deeper sense of his plan for us, but we also become more and more committed to following his design for us. As Christians, we also are joined together in a new community—the church. More than ever before, the potential for dynamic, loving relationships can be realized. We are connected to each other not only as men and women but also as brothers and sisters with the same Father, the same Lord, the same faith, the same hope, and the same love. No wonder the apostle Paul gives us this command: "Therefore, be imitators of God, as dearly loved children. And walk in love, as the Messiah also loved us and gave Himself for us, a sacrificial and fragrant offering to God" (Ephesians 5:1–2).

God designed the church to be the start of the new humanity. Our purpose as followers of Jesus Christ—both individually and together, being created in the image of God—is to reflect him in the world in which we live.

In the next chapter, I'll explain in greater detail how we can imitate God so as to carry out his design for us.

．．．．．．．．．．．．．．．．．．．．．

"Why do I exist?" "Does human existence have meaning?" "What is the purpose for my life?" My pastor and I grabbed a video camera one day and headed down to Hawthorne Street, a haven for alternative shops, alternative lifestyles, and alternative people. We found all types of people—storeowners and homeless people, skin-heads and hippies (yes, my city still has plenty of holdovers from the '60s), atheists and believers, pierced young people and senior citizens, goths and jocks. Once we introduced ourselves, we stuck the video camera in their faces and asked them this question: "If you could ask God any question, what would you ask him?" The second-most popular response (I'll talk about the number one question later) was this: "What is the purpose for my life?"

No matter who people are and what people are like, they want an answer to this question. Perhaps the issue doesn't arise con-sciously very often, but when people reflect on their situation—when they are lonely, at crisis points, when someone has died—they wonder about the purpose of life. And they are not just mildly interested in the response. It's not like an answer they may write on a test or give to some trivia question. The answer is a matter of great importance because they want to figure out the mystery of human existence. They want to know why they exist and if they are ful-filling the purpose for which they exist.

PAUSE TIME— Now that you've read this chapter on the image of God, think carefully how you would answer this question: "What is the purpose for my life?" What does it mean for you to be created in God's image? How does this make you feel? Does this give you a sense of significance, dignity, and pur-pose? When you look at yourself in the mirror, what do you see? Remember: God has made you absolutely unique. No one has ever existed and will ever exist just like you—and that is by God's design. Don't ever be envious or jealous of others! Thank God instead, and live so as to reflect him uniquely in your world.

God's Greatness

Not long after the fall of communism in the former Soviet Union, I was invited to teach a course on church history in St. Petersburg. Knowing how notoriously difficult it was to obtain permission to enter the USSR, I gave myself plenty of time to get all the official documents. An updated American passport was no problem, and my efforts to obtain a visa for Russia seemed to progress well. My sponsoring agency in Russia had sent me an official invitation, and the paperwork was completed, so I packaged it all together with my passport and sent it to the Russian Embassy in Washington, D.C. I bought my airline tickets, sent confirmation of my arrival date and time, and sat back to wait for my visa to arrive.

I figured that no action would be taken for awhile, but with about a week left before I was scheduled to leave, I called the embassy. An immigration official confirmed that my request for a visa had arrived and assured me it would be taken care of promptly. A few days later, panic sunk in when I still had not received my passport. A frantic call caught the attention of another Russian official, who proudly told me that my passport and visa were sitting right in front of him on his desk. He promised to put it in the mail that day. Given that it was Thursday and I was to leave on Saturday, I explained to him that it would never arrive in time. I pleaded with him to express mail it—yes, I would pay the cost—and he agreed to do that.

Saturday morning arrived, but there was no sight of my visa. My suitcases were packed, the tickets were in my hands, and we had to

leave for the airport within the next fifteen minutes or ↙
tainly miss my plane. All we could do at that point was pray
ered the family together, and we got down on our knees. Huᴅ
together, we cried out desperately to God to intervene. Suddenly,
my oldest daughter announced that a deliveryman was walking up
to our house with a package in his hand. Eagerly and with great
unbelief, I grabbed the visa out of his hand. He explained how fortunate we were that he had found us, which confused us. Then he
showed us the address on the package: it was the wrong street, the
wrong city, and the wrong zip code. It was only his persistence in
trying to deliver the package that got it to us in the nick of time.

The drive to the airport that Saturday was a time for great praise
and thanksgiving. Once again, God had proved his greatness.
Sovereign timing and resourcefulness demonstrated that he is a
faithful God who is worthy of our absolute trust.

. . . .

I hope that you have had similar experiences of God's greatness.
In this chapter and the next I focus on the attributes that make him
so great. In what may seem an incredible surprise, we possess these
attributes as well, albeit in a very limited and imperfect way. These
communicable attributes are those that we share with God—or,
better, that he shares with us. Because he created human beings—
you and me—in his image, God shares certain qualities with us so
that we, like a mirror, will reflect him in the world in which we live.

Be Imitators of God

Do you remember Paul's command from the last chapter? "Be
imitators of God, as dearly loved children. And walk in love, as the
Messiah also loved us and gave Himself for us, a sacrificial and fragrant offering to God" (Ephesians 5:1–2). We are commanded to be
imitators of God. In other passages, we are told specifically which
attributes we are to imitate. For example, Peter tells us to imitate the
holiness of God: "As the One who called you is holy, you also are
to be holy in all your conduct; for it is written, 'Be holy, because I

am holy'" (1 Peter 1:15–16). And Jesus gives what seems like an absolutely impossible requirement to carry out: "But I say to you who listen: Love your enemies, do good to those who hate you, bless those who curse you, pray for those who mistreat you" (Luke 6:27–28). He then explains how imitating God is the only way for us to ever obey this command: "Be merciful, just as your Father also is merciful" (Luke 6:36).

Our task is set before us: *first,* to focus on God's greatness and goodness by describing his communicable attributes, and *second,* to consider how we should imitate these attributes in our relationships. These relationships are those we have with our parents, our brothers and sisters, our friends, other Christians, our teachers at school, our employers and customers at work, and so forth. By doing this, we will discover in greater detail how we can concretely imitate God so as to reflect him in the world in which we live. And don't forget: Only by relying on his power and resources will we ever be able to imitate God authentically!

As I have thought about and relived my experience of waiting for my Russian visa, I have become convinced that God knew exactly what he was doing. What is more, God wisely orchestrated the exact circumstances of that episode for his glory and my benefit (though it certainly was confusing and worrisome to me at the time). This means that he acted powerfully to bring about the events, all of which he worked out according to his sovereign plan. Throughout all this, God once again proved himself to be truthful and faithful. In other words, God demonstrated some of the attributes he wants me to imitate: his knowledge, his wisdom, his power, his sovereignty, and his truthfulness and faithfulness. Let's examine each one more closely and see how God shares them with us.

God's Knowledge

I can confidently affirm that God knew what he was doing because he knows everything. God's *omniscience* (remember, *omni* means "all" or "everything" and *science* refers to "knowledge") means that he knows the past, the present, and the future, including all actual things as well as all possible things. The apostle John informs us that God "knows all things" (1 John 3:20). He does not need to remember things by reaching deep into his memory, and God never comes to learn something new by studying or figuring things out. He just knows everything all at once because he is "perfect in knowledge" (Job 37:16) and "his understanding has no limit" (Psalm 147:5).

This means that God knows us and everything about us—our past (all the good things we have done, as well as all our errors, failures, and sins), our present (all that we are currently doing as we trust and obey him), and our future (all that he has planned for us). David talks about this:

O LORD, you have searched me
    and you know me.
You know when I sit and when I rise;
    you perceive my thoughts from afar.
You discern my going out and my lying down;
    you are familiar with all my ways.
Before a word is on my tongue
    you know it completely, O LORD.
You hem me in, behind and before;
    you have laid your hand on me.
Such knowledge is too wonderful for me,
    too lofty for me to attain.
(Psalm 139:1–6)

God knows all the details of our lives: our sleeping, waking, sitting, standing, coming home from school, and going to a party. He knows exactly what we are going to say before we say it—our respectful reply to a parent or boss, our boastful remark to make ourselves look better than we really are, our cutting joke to put another student down, our comforting words to help a friend facing a tragedy. He can know these words before they are spoken because he has full access to our minds and knows every one of our thoughts. He sees through duplicity and knows what is authentic and what is mere show. God knows the motivations behind our actions—whether we do a good deed to draw attention to ourselves or to bring honor to him. He can't be fooled, and he is pleased when we sincerely trust and obey him. God certainly knew my need for a visa, the procrastination at the Russian Embassy, my departure date and time, exactly when I needed to receive the visa, and the concern of the deliveryman who would ultimately give it to me at just the right moment.

God's knowledge extends beyond us to include what is happening with our city, state, country, and all the nations of the world. He has knowledge of the entire universe as well. From the most minute details of our lives—"But even the hairs of your head have all been counted" (Matthew 10:30)—to the outer limits of the universe—"He determines the number of the stars and calls them each by name" (Psalm 147:4)—God knows everything that exists and takes place.

God knows not only the past and present, but the future as well. The church has always believed this, though some Christians now question it. This is disappointing and disturbing because the Bible is very clear about God's all-encompassing knowledge of the future. In fact, one of the challenges that God himself lays down to other so-called gods or idols is to predict accurately the future:

"Bring in your idols to tell us
    what is going to happen.
Tell us what the former things were,
    so that we may consider them and know
    their final outcome.
Or declare to us the things to come,
    tell us what the future holds,
so we may know that you are gods." (Isaiah 41:22–23)

If these idols are true and living gods, they will be able to meet this challenge. This is so because any true and living god knows the future. Of course, these gods fail the test—they are unable to prophesy about what is to come—because they do not know the future. Only our true and living God knows such things:

"I am God, and there is no other;
    I am God, and there is none like me.
I make known the end from the beginning,
    from ancient times, what is still to come."
(Isaiah 46:9–10)

Our God is unlike all other so-called gods because he knows the future. Indeed, God is great because he knows everything!

PAUSE TIME— Imitating God's knowledge: One obvious way that we can imitate God's knowledge is by knowing him better by reading his Word. Reading other books—for example, those in the *TruthQuest* series—can also increase our knowledge about him. But our knowledge should imitate his knowledge even beyond these "spiritual" areas. For example, God knows the inner workings of atomic structure, cell reduplication, chemical bonding, quarks and black holes, electromagnetism, and so forth. As a student, you are in a unique place to imitate God's knowledge by studying biology, chemistry, physics, genetics, astronomy, and other school courses. Both your parents and your teachers play important roles in helping you to know more so as to increase in your imitation of God's knowledge. And you can play a similar role in the lives of others—especially those who don't know God or those who are new believers.

What other ways can you imitate God's knowledge?

God's Wisdom

Beyond his perfect knowledge of my visa situation, God acted with great wisdom throughout the entire episode. God's *wisdom* means that he always chooses the best goals and the best ways to accomplish those goals. Wisdom is far more than mere efficiency, however. Our wise God values the highest good in terms of what will bring him the greatest glory and what is of greatest benefit to us as his children. In his infinite wisdom, God constructs his purpose in keeping with his highest values for his own glory and our greatest good, and the steps he chooses to accomplish his plan are certain to be the very best ways.

The Bible affirms that God is "wise in heart" (Job 9:4 NKJV). When Paul describes God as "the only wise God" (Romans 16:27), he reminds us that this attribute distinguishes God from all other so-called gods. This unique wisdom is displayed in several ways. God employed great wisdom when he created the world, as the following psalm emphasizes:

How many are your works, O LORD!
    In wisdom you make them all;
    the earth is full of your creatures.
There is the sea, vast and spacious,
    teeming with creatures beyond number—
    living things both large and small. (Psalm 104:24–25)

God also was very wise in purposing and accomplishing our salvation. Though the good news about a crucified Jesus sounds stupid to unbelievers, God applied great wisdom in designing his strategy to rescue us. Indeed, God's wisdom confounds human wisdom—which in comparison seems like utter foolishness: "Hasn't God made the world's wisdom foolish? For since, in God's wisdom, the world did not know God through wisdom, God was pleased to save those who believe through the foolishness of the message preached. For the Jews ask for signs and the Greeks seek wisdom, but we preach Christ crucified, a stumbling block to the Jews and foolishness to the Gentiles. Yet to those who are called, both Jews and Greeks, Christ is God's power and God's wisdom, because God's foolishness is wiser than human wisdom, and God's weakness is stronger than human strength" (1 Corinthians 1:20–25). God displays his wisdom in both creation and salvation.

Furthermore, God displays his great wisdom in human lives— yours and mine. In particular, God's wisdom lies at the heart of this very important promise that God gives to us: "We know that all things work together for the good of those who love God: those who are called according to His purpose. For those He foreknew He also predestined to be conformed to the image of His Son, so that He would be the firstborn among many brothers" (Romans 8:28–29).

When it comes to events, circumstances, people, and opportunities that come our way, God's goal is always to accomplish the "good" in our lives. He has defined that "good" as being conformed to the image of Jesus Christ. God's plan is to use all things wisely in our lives to transform us to be more and more like Christ. The goal is the very best one: conformity to the Son of God. And God acts wisely through all aspects of our lives to bring about that very good goal.

We never have to worry whether the events of our lives are designed for evil. Though others may intend to harm us, God always intends to accomplish our good in everything. We never have to fear that the circumstances of our lives are somehow out of control, for God himself is at work through those circumstances. We never have to suffer a sense of despair over the people and opportunities—or lack of opportunities—in our lives. Certainly I would have preferred a smoother, less worrisome pathway to obtain a visa. I did not understand why I had to wait until the very last minute for it to arrive! Yet what an opportunity I had to observe our wise God work out his plan. He *always* acts wisely.

 Imitating God's wisdom: Choose a personal goal that you would like to attain. It could be an athletic goal—decreasing your time for the 5K run or 100-meter backstroke, or increasing your free throw percentage. It could be an academic goal—getting a better grade in math class, or learning more about U.S. history since World War II. It could be a spiritual goal—getting to know some non-Christians better or making progress in overcoming a certain temptation. As you set clear goals, think through the best ways to achieve those goals. Attending a skills-oriented sports camp or increasing your practice time could help with athletic goals. Finding a tutor or reading more in areas of interest could help with academic goals. Being purposeful in making friends with nonbelievers or telling your darkest secrets to a mentor could help with spiritual goals. We imitate God's wisdom whenever we choose good goals and develop concrete ways to achieve those goals.

What other ways can you imitate God's wisdom?

God's Power

In addition to his perfect knowledge and great wisdom, God is great because he is all-powerful. The *omnipotence* of God means that he can do all that he as God is able to do. He created a world when nothing other than he existed. He rescued his people Israel out of slavery in Egypt by parting the Red Sea. He powerfully acted to move my visa through the perpetually slow Russian immigration service into the mail system and ultimately into the hands of just the right deliveryman who would not be deterred by an incorrect address so as to give it to me at just the right moment.

At first glance, we may be tempted to say that God's omnipotence means that God can do everything. But as strange as it may sound, God is not able to do certain things. For example, he is not able to die or in any way cease being God. That is, his power cannot be used to destroy who he is. He cannot lie, he cannot sin, he cannot not know everything, and he cannot do anything that contradicts his attributes. That is, his power cannot be used to detract from himself. He cannot fail to accomplish his plans, nor can he break his promises. Also, God cannot do nonsense, like make a square triangle or create a rock so big that he cannot lift it. Because there are some things that God cannot do— his power is infinite yet qualified by all his attributes—it is better to say that his omnipotence means he can do all that he as God is able to do.

Scripture affirms this attribute both positively and negatively. Negatively, Jeremiah praises God saying, "Nothing is too hard for you" (Jeremiah 32:17). Positively, Jesus notes, "With God all things are possible" (Matthew 19:26). Though the Bible is full of examples of God's power, some particular instances include his creation of the universe (Genesis 1), giving the child Isaac to old Abraham and infertile Sarah (Genesis 18:1–15; 21:1–7), the parting of the waters of the Red Sea (Exodus 14), the conception of Jesus by the virgin Mary (Luke 1:26–38), Christ's miracles, and the mighty coming of the Holy Spirit on the day of Pentecost (Acts 2).

God's power is at work in our lives as we trust and obey him. The apostle Peter assures us of this in a general way: "For His divine power has given us everything required for life and godliness, through the knowledge of Him who called us by His own glory and goodness" (2 Peter 1:3). Specifically, this divine power enables us to overcome any and all temptations that come our way. By relying on the Holy Spirit and the resources he provides, we are able to know and do God's will and not give into our selfish desires. With this in mind, Paul issues this command: "I say then, walk by the Spirit and you will not carry out the desire of the flesh. For the flesh desires what is against the Spirit, and the Spirit desires what is against the flesh; these are opposed to each other, so that you don't do what you want" (Galatians 5:16–17). Paul vividly describes the battle that wages inside of us between the Spirit and our sinful nature. If we follow the Holy Spirit and depend on his power, we will consistently avoid sin and carry out what we really want to do—God's will, not ours. But if we give in and satisfy the desires of our sinful nature, we end up doing our own thing and taking our own way. Because this is not what we really want to do, no wonder we end up feeling guilty, ashamed, dirty, and confused. The good news is, we are not left on our own to overcome temptation. Rather, God's power is available to us as we are guided and empowered by the Holy Spirit.

God's power also equips us for serving Jesus Christ. Before he ascended into heaven, Jesus himself promised his disciples: "You will receive power when the Holy Spirit has come upon you, and you will be My witnesses in Jerusalem, in all Judea and Samaria, and to the ends of the earth" (Acts 1:8).

When we tell others about Jesus Christ, when we teach the Word at a Bible study, when we help other Christians by giving wise counsel, when we organize youth group meetings, when we lead worship—in short, whenever we engage in ministry for Jesus Christ—we are not left alone. Notice how this energized Paul's idea of ministry: "We proclaim Him, warning and teaching everyone with all wisdom, so that we may present everyone mature in Christ. I labor for this, striving with His strength that works powerfully in me" (Colossians 1:28–29). Ministry energized by God's power is how we serve Jesus Christ.

 Imitating God's power: Ask God in prayer to give you an assignment that is too big for you to handle in your own strength. It may have to do with accepting some aspect of your personality or appearance that particularly upsets you. It may be some fear to overcome—delivering a speech in class or asking for help from a teacher or youth leader. It may involve being a mediator between warring friends—or even parents. As you become convinced that this is something that God wants you to work on, ask him for his power and resources to accomplish his will. Imitating his power means you will be able to do what God wants you to do.

What other ways can you imitate God's power?

God's Sovereignty

The knowledge, wisdom, and power that God exercised in my experience with the visa demonstrate that he is absolutely sovereign. The *sovereignty* of God means that he does as he pleases to accomplish all his good will and bring great glory to himself. When we address him as "Lord Almighty" and "King," we acknowledge that God is sovereign. He determines what he wants to do and then rules over everything—each individual person, all the nations, each and every event that occurs—to ensure that his will is accomplished. Throughout all of this, his glory is magnified.

One aspect of God's sovereignty is his will. As our sovereign Lord, God wills or purposes to do certain things. For example, he decided that instead of nothing existing outside of himself, he would create the universe and all that it contains. Because of his sovereign will to create our world, God is continually being praised in heaven:

"Our Lord and God,
You are worthy to receive
glory and honor and power,
because You have created all things,
and because of Your will
they exist and were created." (Revelation 4:11)

Another example of God's sovereign will is the crucifixion of Jesus Christ. Twice in the Book of Acts, this divine decision is the focus of attention. The apostle Peter preached about it: "Jesus the Nazarene was a man pointed out to you by God with miracles, wonders, and signs that God did among you through Him, just as you yourselves know. Though He was delivered up according to God's determined plan and foreknowledge, you used lawless people to nail Him to a cross and kill Him" (Acts 2:22–23). The disciples also praised God for his sovereign purpose: "Herod and Pontius Pilate, with the Gentiles and the peoples of Israel, assembled together against Your holy Servant Jesus, whom You anointed, to do whatever Your hand and Your plan had predestined to take place" (Acts 4:27–28).

Two key facts are presented here: First, evil people acted together in a wicked conspiracy to crucify Jesus Christ. The innocent Son of God was nailed to a cross and put to death, and those who pulled off this travesty of justice are held responsible for their actions. Second, God had planned to allow this evil conspiracy long ago because the crucifixion of his Son accomplished his sovereign will for Jesus Christ to die for our salvation. What happened on the cross was no mere accident; on the contrary, the crucifixion was God's set purpose to rescue us from sin and punishment. His sovereign will was accomplished through a wicked event that saves us and ultimately brings great glory to God.

One final example: God's sovereign will extends to his choice of us to become Christians. The apostle Paul explains this: "[God] predestined us to be adopted through Jesus Christ for Himself, according to His favor and will, to the praise of His glorious grace that He favored us with in the Beloved" (Ephesians 1:5–6). God has predestined, or sovereignly chosen, us to become his adopted children. This choice was not based on how we look, whether or not we are good people, our ability to have faith, our willingness to obey, or anything else about us. Rather, God predestined us according to his own good pleasure (we joyfully delight God's heart by being his sons and daughters) and his will (he decided to adopt us into his family). This sovereign choice came about through Jesus Christ, from whom we receive the grace necessary for salvation.

Ultimately, this results in glory and honor for God, for our only possible response to God's choice of us and his gift of grace to us is praise.

Whatever God has purposed to do, he accomplishes. Speaking with God, Job acknowledged this with great simplicity: "I know that you can do all things; no plan of yours can be thwarted" (Job 42:2). Isaiah uses the image of an outstretched hand to symbolize God's power to accomplish his sovereign purpose:

This is the plan determined for the whole world;
> this is the hand stretched out over all nations.
For the LORD Almighty has purposed, and who can
> thwart him?
His hand is stretched out, and who can turn it back?
(Isaiah 14:26–27)

Talking about God's plan, Paul notes that God "works out everything in agreement with the decision of His will" (Ephesians 1:11). Not some things, but everything; not just the big things, but even the smallest details (including the processing and delivery of a visa)—all things that occur take place in step with what God's sovereign will has purposed to happen.

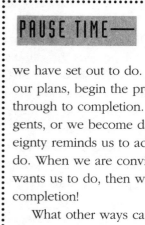

PAUSE TIME— Imitating God's sovereignty: One way of imitating this is to focus our efforts and resources on accomplishing what we have set out to do. Too often we get a great idea, make our plans, begin the project, but then we don't see the task through to completion. We get sidetracked and pursue tangents, or we become discouraged and give up. God's sovereignty reminds us to accomplish what we have purposed to do. When we are convinced that this is something that God wants us to do, then we have a double motivation to see it to completion!

What other ways can you imitate God's sovereignty?

God's Truthfulness and Faithfulness

As our sovereign Lord who is powerfully able to accomplish his good and wise plan, God proves himself to be truthful and faithful. The *truthfulness* and *faithfulness* of God (these words are somewhat different) mean that he always tells the truth and always fulfills what he promises. Paul affirms that God does not lie (Titus 1:2). The writer to the Hebrews goes even further: "It is impossible for God to lie" (Hebrews 6:18). Whenever God speaks, he always tells the truth. This attribute gives us great confidence that everything that Scripture affirms is completely truthful. Whether the Bible addresses matters relating to our salvation and faith—the person and work of Jesus Christ, the ministries of the Holy Spirit, how to worship God, the importance of trust and obedience—or matters related to history, genealogies, creation, and so forth, it is completely true. Because God is truthful and his Word is wholly true, David is able to pray: "O Sovereign LORD, you are God! Your words are trustworthy" (2 Samuel 7:28). We can count on God because he is absolutely reliable.

God is also faithful, always fulfilling what he promises. We have already seen that God is unchanging in regard to his promises:

God is not a man, that he should lie,

nor a son of man, that he should change his mind.

Does he speak and then not act?

Does he promise and not fulfill? (Numbers 23:19)

The answer to these questions is "No. Of course not!" God does not commit himself to something and then go back on his promise. This is also because he is a faithful God.

God has promised many things in Scripture, and he can be relied upon to fulfill those promises. Of greatest importance is his promise of eternal life to all those who call Jesus Christ their Savior and Lord. In light of this, the writer to the Hebrews offers this encouragement: "Let us hold on to the confession of our hope without wavering, for He who promised is faithful" (Hebrews 10:23). Once God has started his work in our life through Jesus Christ, he will always be faithful and never abandon what he began. Speaking of this, Paul tells us to be "sure of this, that He who started a good work in you will carry it on to completion until the day of Christ Jesus" (Philippians 1:6).

As I faced the puzzling possibility that my visa would not arrive in time, I was comforted by God's truthfulness and faithfulness. I was certain that he had directed me to engage in ministry in Russia. At each step of the way, God had opened the necessary doors for me to go. But then I was stuck—no visa. I either had to leave in fifteen minutes to catch my plane or completely abandon my trip. I grasped onto his promises: "But seek first the kingdom of God and His righteousness, and all these things [—even a visa!—] will be provided for you" (Matthew 6:33). Also: "My God will supply all your needs according to His riches in glory in Christ Jesus" (Philippians 4:19). God proved himself absolutely reliable by fulfilling his promises. Certainly he is truthful and faithful!

 **PAUSE TIME—** Imitating God's truthfulness and faithfulness: Are you a person who says one thing but means another? Do you keep your promises? If someone shares something with you in strict confidentiality, do you tell that secret to others? Do you stretch the truth to make yourself look better in the eyes of others? Do you think that being humble means that you shouldn't truthfully tell about the abilities and talents God has given you, so you understate your accomplishments? Are you faithful in keeping the commitments you make? For example, if you tell friends you will meet them at a certain time, are you punctual? If you tell kids at youth group you will pray for them, does God hear from you about them? If you say you'll come to a certain party but then get a better offer, do you forego the first in favor of the second?

What other ways can you imitate God's truthfulness and faithfulness?

God's Goodness

Not long after I committed my life to Jesus Christ, I had the opportunity to help organize an outreach featuring a talk entitled "The Resurrection: Fact or Fiction?" We received permission to hold the event in a free-speech area at a university, so we arranged the stage, set up a large wooden cross, prayed together for the talk, then went off to eat some lunch before the event began. Upon our return, we were shocked: some satanists had trashed our stage by turning the cross upside down and stationing black candles all around the area. This turned out to be a relatively minor nuisance, however. As soon as the speaker got up to the platform, atheists in the large crowd began to curse at him and taunt him. Because I was new to Christianity, I had never seen anything quite like this before. Naively, I approached one of the most vocal hecklers and invited him to come and talk with me away from the area so the speaker wouldn't be disturbed. With one hand grabbing me roughly by my shirt collar, he thrust the other hand in my face and threatened, "If you say one more #*&!#&* word, I'll cram this fist down your throat!" Though certainly frightened, I immediately thought, *This Christianity must be the real thing because I'm being persecuted for believing it!*

• •

How do you think God felt about this incident? Christians attempted to share the good news about Jesus Christ and were harassed by satanists and threatened physically by atheists so that the message would be drowned out. In this chapter I will focus on some of God's other communicable attributes that come out of this story—attributes that demonstrate that he is very good.

God's Love

As I think about it, one of the key reasons we organized that outreach was the love of God. In fact, this love motivated us to risk our own safety for the sake of others in a way that parallels Jesus Christ's sacrifice of his own life for our sake.

God's *love* means that he always gives himself and his good gifts to benefit others. "God is love" (1 John 4:8), the apostle John tells us. Before God created the world and human beings to love, God was characterized by dynamic, loving relationships between the Father, the Son, and the Holy Spirit. Thus, the Father always loves the Son, the Son always loves the Father, the Father always loves the Spirit, and so forth. This reciprocal loving relationship with the Father was so important to Jesus that he spoke several times about it shortly before his death. At one point he told the disciples: "I am going away so that the world may know that I love the Father. Just as the Father commanded Me, so I do" (John 14:31). A bit later, when praying to the Father for his disciples, Jesus again underscored this love: "Father, I desire those You have given Me to be with Me where I am. Then they may see My glory, which You have given Me because You loved Me before the world's foundation. Righteous Father! The world has not known You. However, I have known You, and these have known that You sent Me. I made Your name known to them and will make it known, so that the love with which You have loved Me may be in them, and that I may be in them" (John 17:24–26). Clearly, the eternal relationship of love that the Son enjoyed with the Father was a primary motivation for Jesus to sacrifice his own life so that others— you and I—could have a relationship of love with God as well.

The Bible often focuses on love as the basis for the death of Christ. Jesus himself noted, "No one has greater love than this, that someone would lay down his life for his friends" (John 15:13). John explains in his gospel: "For God loved the world in this way: He gave His only Son, so that everyone who believes in Him will not perish but have eternal life" (John 3:16). The cross stands as the greatest testimony to God's love for us—not his love for us as his friends and followers, but his love for us as sinners and enemies: "For while we were still helpless, at the appointed moment, Christ died for the ungodly. For rarely will someone die for a just person—though for a good person perhaps someone might even dare to die. But God proves His own love for us in that while we were still sinners Christ died for us!" (Romans 5:6–8).

God's love is a self-initiating love. It doesn't consider the identity of its object, nor does it wait for the one who is loved to make the first move. As John notes: "God's love was revealed among us in this way: God sent His only Son into the world so that we might live through Him. Love consists in this: not that we loved God, but that He loved us and sent His Son to be the propitiation for our sins" (1 John 4:9–10). God's love takes the initiative to reach out to us and does not depend on us making ourselves loveable. Because it is of this nature, we can count on God's love being constant toward us. As the words of one song put it:

He loves us with passion, without regret.

He cannot love more and will not love less.[1]

Because of this constant love, we also reach out to others with the good news of Jesus Christ.

 Imitating God's love: Sometimes imitating God's love means strengthening the relationships we already have. As you think through those relationships—with parents, brothers and sisters, friends, people at church, employers, and colleagues at work—do any strike you as needing to be renewed? Is your love in those relationships a self-sacrificing, constant, initiating love? Imitating God's love may also involve reaching out to others—those with whom we have no current relationship, even those whom we find unlovable. Should imitating God's love lead you to establish a relationship with someone new? In what way can God's love motivate you today to share the good news with someone else?

What other ways can you imitate God's love?

God's Righteousness and Justice

In addition to his love being an important factor in our outreach, God's justice or righteousness motivated us as well. The *righteousness* or *justice* of God—I will use these words interchangeably—means that he always does what is right and that his judgment of what his creatures do is fair. Indeed, God himself determines what is right and wrong, and he judges his creatures according to the standard that he has established.

Moses affirms the justice of God:

"He is the Rock, his works are perfect,
  and all his ways are just.
A faithful God who does no wrong,
  upright and just is he." (Deuteronomy 32:4)

This attribute of righteousness reinforces the promise that we have already considered: "We know that all things work together for the good of those who love God: those who are called according to His purpose" (Romans 8:28). Because God is righteous, we can always count on him to do right in the events and circumstances of our life. He never makes a mistake (his wisdom guarantees this as well), and he works righteously through everything that occurs in our lives to bring about his design. Though his ways may puzzle us and at times seem unfair and even wrong—think about suffering and deep tragedy, for example—we can trust that even in these desperate times, God continues to act righteously toward us.

Just as the cross demonstrates God's love, the greatest proof of God's justice is the death of Jesus Christ. Paul explains: "God presented Him as a propitiation through faith in His blood, to demonstrate His righteousness, because in His restraint God passed over the sins previously committed. He presented Him to demonstrate His righteousness at the present time, so that He would be righteous and declare righteous the one who has faith in Jesus" (Romans 3:25–26). When Christ died on the cross, his death was a sacrifice of atonement—it paid the penalty of the death that we deserved because of our sins. Previous to this death, God had not fully dealt with the sins of the people living before Christ. He was waiting for the cross, at which time the death of Christ would pay the penalty for all people—those who lived before him, those present during his earthly ministry, and all those who would come after Christ lived, like you and me. By the death of Christ, God proved he is just because he did punish sin. As a righteous God, he must give people what they deserve. Because sin deserves punishment, God must punish sinful people. Through the death of Christ on the cross, God did indeed deal with sin—not by punishing us, but by punishing his own Son in our place. So God remains just—he did not relax the penalty due to sin, but made sure the penalty was paid. Then when we trust Christ by faith, God justifies us—he declares us not guilty, but righteous instead. He does so because the penalty has been paid, and he gives us the gift of Christ's righteousness. Throughout all of this, God demonstrates that he is a perfectly just God.

But what about those who don't trust Christ by faith and receive this gift of Christ's righteousness? Because God is just, he must judge people by the standard he has established. Paul emphasizes this: "It is righteous for God to repay with affliction those who afflict you, . . . taking vengeance with flaming fire on those who don't know God and on those who don't obey the gospel of our Lord Jesus. These will pay the penalty of everlasting destruction, away from the Lord's presence and from His glorious strength" (2 Thessalonians 1:6, 8–9). All those who reject the good news of Jesus Christ face a dreadful future of eternal punishment. In acting toward them in this way, God proves that he is righteous because he gives people what they deserve for their choice of rebellion and sin. Again, Paul warns these people: "But because of your hardness and unrepentant heart you are storing up wrath for yourself in the day of wrath, when God's righteous judgment is revealed. He will repay each one according to his works: eternal life to those who by patiently doing good seek for glory, honor, and immortality; but wrath and indignation to those who are self-seeking and disobey the truth, but are obeying unrighteousness" (Romans 2:5–8). As I will explain more fully in a bit, God's wrath—his intense hatred of sin that leads to punishment—will be poured out on sinful, self-seeking, evil people. This must be the case, because God is perfectly just.

The justice of God becomes another key motivation for us to tell others about Jesus Christ. Apart from hearing the good news and trusting Jesus Christ, people are without hope and will face a terrible future. We communicate the gospel so that others can discover and lay hold of Jesus Christ and be justified by our righteous God.

Even for us Christians, the righteousness of God means that he will one day evaluate all that we do, think, and say during our present life. This will not be an evaluation to determine whether or not we will receive the gift of eternal life. That issue was already decided when God justified us as we trusted Jesus Christ as Savior and Lord. Paul assures us, "Therefore, no condemnation now exists for those in Christ Jesus" (Romans 8:1). Rather, we will face God's judgment for how we have lived our lives. Paul describes this evaluation: "For we must all appear before the judgment seat of Christ, so that each may be repaid for what he has done in the body, whether good or bad" (2 Corinthians 5:10). In keeping with his righteousness, God will reward us for the good things we have done, but we will lose our potential reward for the wrong things we have done. This future evaluation should motivate us to live our lives with constant trust and obedience while we avoid all that displeases God.

PAUSE TIME — Imitating God's righteousness or justice: Are you known as a just person? Do others regard you as a person of integrity—that is, as a person who holds to a certain standard and upholds that standard in both his personal life and in his treatment of others? Sometimes there is a total disconnect between a person's private world and public persona. Do you wear a mask when you're with others—you play the kind of person you think they want you to be—but when you're alone you are completely different? How can you imitate God's righteousness so as to overcome this schizophrenic lifestyle?

What other ways can you imitate God's righteousness or justice?

God's Holiness and Jealousy

Earlier I asked a question about how God must have felt about what the satanists and atheists did at our outreach. Because he is holy and jealous, God was deeply disturbed by their attempts to disrupt our communication of the good news. God's *holiness* means that he is greatly exalted above everything else and, because he is completely pure and separated from sin, he resists all who are an affront to him and his ways.

Isaiah describes our holy God:

Do you not know?

Have you not heard?

Has it not been told you from the beginning?

Have you not understood since the earth was founded?

He sits enthroned above the circle of the earth,

and its people are like grasshoppers.

He stretches out the heavens like a canopy,

and spreads them out like a tent to live in.

He brings princes to naught

and reduces the rulers of this world to nothing.

No sooner are they planted,

no sooner are they sown,

no sooner do they take root in the ground,

than he blows on them and they wither,

and a whirlwind sweeps them away like chaff.

"To whom will you compare me?

Or who is my equal?" says the Holy One. (Isaiah 40:21–25)

The princes and rulers of this world represent all that is proud and lifted up against God and his sovereign purposes. The Holy One, who has no equivalent in heaven or on earth, views them as mere grasshoppers and easily blows them into nothingness. As Habakkuk says to God, "Your eyes are too pure to look on evil; you cannot tolerate wrong" (Habakkuk 1:13). God's displeasure was provoked by the satanists and atheists who wickedly opposed his way to reach out to others.

God also was displeased because he is jealous. The *jealousy* of God means that he rightly guards his own honor. Because he and he alone is the incomparable God, he will not share the honor that is due him with anyone or anything else. When we as people made in his image give our heart to something other than God—when we set our affection on our own popularity, our own pleasures, our own way—God becomes jealous.

It may seem very strange to say that God is jealous. In most cases, the jealousy we know and experience is more like envy. Someone may be more beautiful or handsome, more popular or talented, more athletic or intelligent than we are, so we become jealous or envious of that other person. In the end, we want something that does not rightly belong to us—a better body, a better personality, or better abilities. This kind of jealousy is wrong. But there is a right kind of jealousy as well. For example, think about the relationship you enjoy with your best friend. Imagine that someone attempts to come between the two of you and break that relationship apart. Perhaps the intruder's attempts focus on tearing you down—telling lies about you and slandering your character. Perhaps this outsider forces himself or herself on your best friend—constantly calling and always hanging around. You would be right to be jealous in this situation. That is, you would be right to defend your own honor and to do whatever it takes to make sure your best friend is not deceived and dominated by this intruder.

So it is with the jealousy of God. Because he and he alone is worthy of our complete devotion, he is rightly jealous of anyone and anything that attempts to rob him of his honor and to steal our undivided attention away from him. This is why God despises idolatry—the worship of other gods—whether that misplaced affection takes the form of love of money, love of pleasure, love of comfort, love of human recognition, or any other inferior love.

We have seen that the Bible has strong warnings against making idols or putting anyone or anything above God in our life: "You shall not make for yourself an idol in the form of anything in heaven above or on the earth beneath or in the waters below. You shall not bow down to them or worship them" (Exodus 20:4–5). Immediately after giving this commandment, Moses explains God's reason for it: "For I, the LORD your God, am a jealous God" (Exodus

20:5). We must never allow anything—our desire for popularity, our search for significance, our need to love and to be loved, our physical passions—or anyone—parents, brothers and sisters, best friends, teachers—to ever claim first place in our lives. We must reserve that space for God and God alone. Otherwise, we must face his jealousy. As God himself says:

> For my own sake, for my own sake, I do this.
> How can I let myself be defamed?
> I will not yield my glory to another. (Isaiah 48:11)

Our holy and jealous God stands opposed to anything and everything that is an affront to him and his sovereign purpose.

PAUSE TIME— Imitating God's holiness and jealousy: There was a woman who had a very interesting and practical approach to imitating God's holiness and jealousy. She was disturbed by her colleagues' vain use of the name of Jesus at her office. Because she wanted to be jealous for God's honor and protect his holiness, she announced to her colleagues that every time they shout out "Jesus!" in anger or frustration, she would yell "is Lord!" Within an hour of her announcement, she heard someone cry, "Jesus!" to which she quickly added "is Lord." A bit later, another shout of "Jesus!" was finished by "is Lord." After a week of increasingly less frequent "Jesus is Lord" proclamations, the office stopped using the Lord's name in vain. Protective of God's honor, this woman creatively imitated his holiness and jealousy at work.

What other ways can you imitate God's jealousy?

God's Mercy and Grace

Despite their efforts to disrupt our outreach, the satanists and atheists did not prevail that day. Our speaker made it completely through his talk on the resurrection and finished up with an explanation of the good news about Jesus Christ. Now I don't know the results of that event—I was too busy with my rough new "friend" to remember much! But I want you to think about how God was present at that meeting.

On the one hand, he was present as our merciful and gracious God. The *mercy* and *grace* of God—these two words are somewhat different—mean that God expresses his goodness to those in disastrous situations and to those who deserve punishment. Mercy reminds us that our God is deeply compassionate—when we lose our way, when we are overwhelmed with problems, he personally feels our distress and moves to rescue us. For example, Isaiah describes the people of Israel in times of trouble and emphasizes God's mercy:

"In all their distress he too was distressed, . . .
In his love and mercy he redeemed them;
    he lifted them up and carried them
    all the days of old." (Isaiah 63:9)

God is keenly aware of the heartache we experience, and in his mercy he feels our disappointment. This is also seen in the ministry of Jesus, who often was approached by beggars, the sick, the blind, the lame, and the dying. They desperately cried out, "Lord, have mercy on us!" Seeing people who were "weary and worn out, like sheep without a shepherd," Jesus felt compassion—he was moved deeply to do something to relieve their distress (Matthew 9:36). God is merciful in helping those in disastrous situations.

God's grace is his goodness in not giving us what we deserve. It is especially seen in his work of salvation. Though we stand guilty before God and condemned because of our sin, he is good toward us in his grace. As Paul explains: "For all have sinned and fall short of the glory of God. They are justified freely by His grace through the redemption that is in Christ Jesus" (Romans 3:23–24). We cannot save ourselves, so in no sense can we ever earn God's love. In place of human effort, God freely justifies us—he declares us not guilty but righteous instead—by an act of his grace. Paul emphasizes this again: "For by grace you are saved through faith, and this is not from yourselves; it is God's gift—not from works, so that no one can boast" (Ephesians 2:8–9).

The only reason that we have been rescued from sin and a terrible future judgment is God's grace. This removes any possibility of pride and boasting on our part because we cannot earn grace by our good works. The only response to grace is to receive that gift of God's love through faith in Jesus Christ.

At our outreach, God was present as our merciful and gracious God. The very fact that we talked about Jesus Christ communicated his mercy and grace to students confused about their lives, couples experiencing relationship difficulties and breakups, others who were disheartened by challenging and frightening circumstances out of their control, and so forth. Even the satanists and atheists, if they were attentive, could have heard of God's mercy and grace for them. For they were not excluded from his goodness. Indeed, God's mercy and grace is designed especially for those who are far away, to bring them back to him forever.

PAUSE TIME— Imitating God's mercy and grace: Currently, do you know anyone in a disastrous situation to whom you can express mercy? It could be a new student at school who is struggling to connect, a friend whose parents have recently divorced, a senior citizen at church who is widowed, or a homeless person who needs food and blankets. How can you mobilize others to join you in imitating God's goodness?

What other ways can you imitate God's mercy and grace?

God's Wrath

On the other hand, God was present at our outreach as our patiently wrathful God. The *wrath* of God means he intensely hates all sin to the point that he is ready to punish it to the fullest extent. This attribute is difficult to talk about because it is one that we hope no one ever experiences. The Bible, however, has a good deal to say about it, and we would not want God to be different—that is, not wrathful.

God's wrath is provoked whenever and wherever there is deep and persistent sin against him. For example, even after the people of Israel had been rescued out of Egypt, crossed the Red Sea, received the Ten Commandments, and witnessed many miracles, they built a golden calf and worshiped this idol as their god. This senseless rebellion ignited God's furious wrath: "'I have seen these people,' the LORD said to Moses, 'and they are a stiff-necked people. Now leave me alone so that my anger may burn against them and that I may destroy them'" (Exodus 32:9–10). God was so righteously upset at his people's foolishness that he was ready to punish their sin to the fullest extent—by completely wiping them off the face of the earth. Had Moses not intervened by praying for God to change his mind, the people of Israel would have been destroyed. Instead of learning from this, however, the people continued to provoke God's wrath. When several leaders challenged the authority of Moses, God burned with righteous anger and destroyed them. When the Israelites complained about this punishment, God began to destroy the people through a plague. Had someone not intervened, many more than the nearly fifteen thousand people who had died would have been destroyed by the divine wrath (see Numbers 16).

Now that Jesus Christ has come, the situation has intensified with regard to God's wrath. Certainly, Christ has come to rescue us from divine wrath: "For God loved the world in this way: He gave His only Son, so that everyone who believes in Him will not perish but have eternal life. For God did not send His Son into the world that He might judge the world, but that the world might be saved through Him" (John 3:16–17). But this escape applies only to those who embrace Jesus. For those who reject him, the dreadful wrath of God and divine condemnation have already begun: "Anyone who believes in Him is not judged, but anyone who does not believe is already judged, because he has not believed in the name of the only Son of God. . . . The one who believes in the Son has eternal life, but the one who refuses to believe in the Son will not see life; instead, the wrath of God remains on him" (John 3:18, 36).

At times, people experience God's wrath even while they are alive. Paul notes that "God's wrath is revealed from heaven against all godlessness and unrighteousness of people who by their unrighteousness suppress the truth" (Romans 1:18). God gives sinful people an initial taste of his wrath by allowing them to reap the bitter consequences of their wickedness. At the same time, they are "storing up wrath for [themselves] in the day of wrath, when God's righteous judgment is revealed" (Romans 2:5). Still, the wrath of God is most often presented as a future experience awaiting the wicked. Paul warns: "For know and recognize this: no sexually immoral or impure or greedy person, who is an idolater, has an inheritance in the kingdom of the Messiah and of God. Let no one deceive you with empty arguments, for because of these things God's wrath is coming on the disobedient" (Ephesians 5:5–6).

A different future awaits us: We believers will never have to face the wrath of God. This is because of the grace and mercy of Jesus Christ, "who rescues us from the coming wrath" (1 Thessalonians 1:10). "Since we have now been declared righteous by His blood, we will be saved through Him from wrath" (Romans 5:9). Because of our escape from divine wrath, we must make a clean break from our former way of life: "Put to death whatever in you is worldly: sexual immorality, impurity, lust, evil desire, and greed, which is idolatry. Because of these, God's wrath comes on the disobedient, and you once walked in these things when you were living in them. But now you must also put away all the following: anger, wrath, malice, slander, and filthy language from your mouth" (Colossians 3:5–8).

Why doesn't God just pour out his wrath quickly and all at once upon everyone who deserves it? Though he intensely hates all sin to the point that he is ready to punish it to the fullest extent, God is also patient. Psalm 103 reminds us:

The LORD is compassionate and gracious,
> slow to anger, abounding in love.
He will not always accuse,
> nor will he harbor his anger forever. (vv. 8–9)

Though ready to express his wrath, God often delays doing so. A key reason is to give more people a chance to turn back to him. Paul leads unbelievers to this conclusion: "Or do you despise the riches of His kindness, restraint, and patience, not recognizing that God's kindness is intended to lead you to repentance?"

(Romans 2:4). As God is patient, his kindness in tolerating sin and not pouring out his wrath is intended to have a beneficial effect on people. Another key reason for this is to give us Christians more time to share the good news of Jesus Christ. Peter tells the church: "The Lord does not delay His promise, as some understand delay, but is patient with you, not wanting any to perish, but all to come to repentance" (2 Peter 3:9). God's patience opens up many more opportunities for us to tell everyone about Christ. That is why we were risking our own safety and experiencing persecution as we tried to reach out to others with the good news. Yes, God is wrathful, standing ready to punish sin to the fullest extent possible. But his heart of love and grace delays carrying out the sentence of punishment because he doesn't want even one person to face eternal punishment. He longs for each and every person to turn from sin and embrace Jesus Christ. Both his impending wrath and his tolerant patience challenge us to spread the gospel and so fulfill the desire of God's heart.

PAUSE TIME— Imitating God's wrath: How can we intensely hate sin while we still love the people who engage in it? Are you convinced that people who don't turn from their sin will face a future of eternal punishment as they experience the wrath of God? Are you convinced that their only hope of escape is to hear the good news of Jesus Christ and embrace him as their Savior and Lord? If you are so convinced, what should you do as a result?

What other ways can you imitate God's wrath?

The Glory of God

Here is the greatness and goodness of God: He is all-knowing, completely wise, powerful in every way, constantly loving, perfectly holy, righteously just, jealous, truthful and faithful, absolutely sovereign, merciful and gracious, and patiently wrathful. We could not ask for anything more or greater, for God is absolutely perfect. He does not lack anything—even the smallest part of any one quality—that is desirable for him to have as God. Rather, he possesses all the excellent qualities in infinite measure so as to be all that he as God should be.

Because of this absolute perfection, God is fully blessed—he takes complete delight in his infinite excellence. Imagine what it would be like to be totally pleased with who you are—your gender, your appearance, your height and weight and body type, your talents and abilities, your goals and motivations, your thoughts and activities—everything. God's contentment with himself infinitely eclipses the greatest joy you could ever experience in being completely pleased with yourself! He is all that he as God should be, and he takes pleasure in who he is. But God also finds delight in us when we reflect him in the world in which we live. Though almost impossible to grasp, we can give God pleasure when we praise and honor him, when we trust and obey him—when we authentically live as people created in his image.

Because he is who he is, God is gloriously beautiful. God's glory is the brilliant radiance that surrounds him because of his majesty. Speaking to God, David commends people who "will speak of the glorious splendor of your majesty" (Psalm 145:5). The awesome radiance of the sun shimmering with intense brightness pales in comparison with the glory of God. It is this glory that people saw when God appeared to them. It is this glory that shone from the tabernacle and temple—the place or sanctuary of God's presence—in Old Testament times. As Psalm 96 notes: "Splendor and majesty are before God; strength and glory are in his sanctuary" (v. 6). With God's special presence in that place, it is no surprise that David prayed:

One thing I ask of the LORD,
    this is what I seek;
that I may dwell in the house of the LORD
    all the days of my life,
to gaze upon the beauty of the LORD
    and to seek him in his temple. (Psalm 27:4)

As believers in Jesus Christ, we no longer worship God in a tabernacle or temple—nor even necessarily in a church building. Rather, we have access to him anywhere and everywhere. Because he is all that he as God should be, the Lord is gloriously beautiful. The deepest desire of our heart should be to seek our God with the eyes of faith and see him in his glorious splendor. We should be captivated by his beauty so that everything else—popularity, ability, recognition, money, comfort, pleasure—pales in comparison, loses its attraction, and ultimately fades away. As one song puts it:

This is the air I breathe
This is the air I breathe
Your holy presence living in me
And I, I'm desperate for you
And I, I'm lost without you[2]

The glorious beauty of the presence of God in our lives is the one and only gift that sustains us and gives our lives meaning. Without this, we are desperately lost and hopeless. With this, we ourselves become beautiful and reflect God's glory to the world around us.

The Mystery of the Trinity

CHAPTER 8

I remember the conversation very well. The person talking with me had been raised in a Christian church but had left it quite awhile before. Since that time, he had become a Jehovah's Witness, quit that and followed a New Age philosophy, and most recently had converted to Islam. He kept pounding away at the Christian belief in the Trinity.

"You Christians believe that the Father is God, right?"

"Right," I replied.

He drew one circle on a piece of paper and wrote the word "Father" in the middle of it. Under this circle he wrote the number "1."

"And you Christians believe that Jesus Christ the Son is God, right?"

"Right again," I answered.

He drew a second circle near the first one and wrote the word "Son" in the middle of it. Again he wrote the number "1" under this circle.

"And you Christians believe that the Holy Spirit is God, right?"

"Once again, you're right," I said.

He drew a third and final circle near the other two and wrote the words "Holy Spirit" in the middle of it. And again he wrote the number "1" under this circle.

Smiling, he performed a simple math problem:

$1 + 1 + 1 = 3$

With a look of victory on his face, he stated his conclusion: "If you Christians believe that the Father is God, and the Son is God, and the Holy Spirit is God, then you believe in three gods! But both the Bible and the *Qur'an*—the holy book of Islam—affirm there is only one God. So you are wrong!"

Taking the pencil from my new friend, I drew a triangle. At the top point I wrote "Father," at the lower left point I wrote "Son," and at the opposite right point I wrote "Holy Spirit." Then I attempted to explain my drawing.

"We Christians do not believe in three gods, but only one God. In my drawing, this one God is represented by the triangle. At each of the points, I wrote three expressions signifying three persons. I don't mean by this that one third of God is the Father, a second third is the Son, and the final third is the Holy Spirit. Rather, all that God is, the Father is; all that God is, the Son is; and all that God is, the Holy Spirit is. And I don't mean to indicate that there are three gods. Rather, we Christians believe that there is one God who eternally exists as three persons—the Father, the Son, and the Holy Spirit. This is the Trinity."

"So $1 + 1 + 1$ does equal 3 for you!" cried my friend.

"No," I responded. "$1 + 1 + 1 = 1$, because the ones of the left side of the equation refer to the number of persons of the Trinity, and the number on the right side refers to the one God."

"But that is terrible math!" my friend complained.

"Yes it is!" I admitted. "But it is great theology, accurately summing up what the Bible teaches about the Trinity."

• •

If you have ever talked with someone about the Trinity, your conversation may have followed the same course as mine. It is very difficult to explain what we Christians believe; it may be even more difficult to understand. But this belief distinguishes Christianity from all other religions. It also lays a firm foundation for dynamic, loving relationships in the Christian community. So though it is very difficult to understand and explain, the doctrine of the Trinity is very important to believe.

In one sense, we shouldn't be surprised by the fact that the Trinity is such a difficult concept to grasp. When we talk about the Trinity, we are attempting to describe the very essence of God himself—literally, the "three-in-oneness" of God. We move beyond a rehearsal of God's works and even go beyond a discussion of God's attributes. When we speak about the Trinity, we are trying to describe God as he is in himself.

What Scripture Reveals about the Trinity

Some people, of course, say that it is impossible to know anything about the essence of God. But Scripture does give us a glimpse of what God is like in himself, and so the doctrine of the Trinity attempts to summarize from the Bible what God reveals about his inner being. Certainly, there is much more to God than he reveals about himself in his Word. As Moses notes: "The secret things belong to the LORD our God, but the things revealed belong to us and to our children forever, that we may follow all the words of this law" (Deuteronomy 29:29).

Try as we might, we can never know the secret things about God. At best, we can only speculate about the things God has not revealed to us in the Bible. But God does reveal some things in his Word about his very essence, so we are on solid ground when we seek to explain and understand the Trinity. What we discover may be hard to understand and explain, and perhaps we come away wishing we could know more. But the fact that we can gain some insight into the mystery of God's very being should lead us to careful study mixed with great praise as we consider the Trinity.

Old Testament

The very first chapter of the Bible gives us a hint about the Trinity. As we have noted, before God actually created us human beings, he deliberated among himself: "Let us make man in our image, in our likeness, and let them rule over the fish of the sea and the birds of the air, over the livestock, over all the earth, and over all the creatures that move along the ground" (Genesis 1:26).

The plural pronouns *us* and *our* indicate that God is more than a solitary being. He is at least two persons; otherwise, such divine conversation could not occur. Elsewhere in the Old Testament, other hints at a plurality of persons in God are found. For example, two people are called "God" in Psalm 45:

Your throne, O God, will last for ever and ever;
   a scepter of justice will be the scepter of your kingdom.
You love righteousness and hate wickedness;
   therefore God, your God, has set you above your companions. (Psalm 45:6–7)

The person who is addressed is called "God," and as a result of his justice, righteousness, and wrath, he is rewarded by a second person who is called "God, your God." We learn later on that this first person is none other than the Son of God (Hebrews 1:8). In another psalm, David writes,

The LORD says to my Lord:
   "Sit at my right hand
until I make your enemies
   a footstool for your feet." (Psalm 110:1)

According to Jesus (Matthew 22:41–46), David calls one person "my Lord," and this person in addressed by another person who is also called "Lord." In other words, God the Father addresses God the Son. These are strong Old Testament indications of a plurality of persons in God.

New Testament

This revelation of the Trinity becomes more clear and complete in the New Testament. At the baptism of Jesus, we see three divine persons at work:

After Jesus was baptized, He went up immediately from the water. The heavens suddenly opened for Him, and He saw

the Spirit of God descending like a dove and coming down
on Him. And there came a voice from heaven:
"This is My beloved Son.
I take delight in Him!" (Matthew 3:16–17)

The Father speaks from heaven, the Son is singled out for the
Father's commendation while being baptized, and the Holy Spirit
descends on the Son to initiate his ministry. At the close of his ministry, Jesus himself links the three together again in instituting
Christian baptism: "All authority has been given to Me in heaven
and on earth. Go, therefore, and make disciples of all nations, baptizing them in the name of the Father and of the Son and of the
Holy Spirit, teaching them to observe everything I have commanded you. And remember, I am with you always, to the end of
the age" (Matthew 28:18–20).

Baptism, therefore, is into the name of the three persons of the
Trinity—the Father, the Son, and the Holy Spirit. The work of God in
choosing us to be his children is ultimately the work of all three persons of the Trinity, as Peter explains: "According to the foreknowledge of God the Father and set apart by the Spirit for obedience and
for the sprinkling with the blood of Jesus Christ" (1 Peter 1:2).

Finally, Paul prays a blessing on us, and this blessing acknowledges the work of the Trinity: "The grace of the Lord Jesus Christ,
and the love of God, and the fellowship of the Holy Spirit be with
all of you" (2 Corinthians 13:13).

From the hints found in the Old Testament, and from the clearer
and more complete revelation in the New Testament, we discover
that God is in reality three persons—the Father, the Son, and the
Holy Spirit.

The Doctrine of the Trinity

Put in a simple form, the doctrine of the Trinity consists of three
affirmations:

1. God eternally exists as three distinct persons—the Father, the
    Son, and the Holy Spirit.
2. Each of these persons is fully God—the Father is fully God,
    the Son is fully God, and the Holy Spirit is fully God.
3. There is only one God.

As we will discover, each of these three affirmations is essential for us to believe.

Affirmation 1: God Eternally Exists as Three Distinct Persons

The first affirmation of Trinitarian doctrine focuses on the fact that the Father, the Son, and the Holy Spirit are different from each other. The Father is not the Son, and the Son is not the Father. The Father is not the Holy Spirit, and the Spirit is not the Father. The Son is not the Holy Spirit, and the Spirit is not the Son. There are two main reasons why it is necessary to maintain these distinctions.

1. Believing the three persons are distinct from each other helps us understand certain biblical passages. For example, at the baptism of Jesus, the Father, the Son, and the Holy Spirit are present and engage in different actions. This would be impossible if they were not distinct persons. Also, John tells us: "In the beginning was the Word; and the Word was with God, and the Word was God. He was with God in the beginning" (John 1:1–2).

The Word—the Son of God, Jesus Christ—is not only fully God; he is also *with* God, meaning he is distinct from the Father. During his earthly ministry, when Jesus prays to the Father, he is truly addressing another person; he is not praying to himself. And Jesus himself promised that the Holy Spirit would be sent by the Father and the Son as "another Counselor" (John 14:16; 15:26)—a distinct person to take his place and continue his ministry. The Father, the Son, and the Holy Spirit are distinct persons.

2. Understanding that God eternally exists as three distinct persons also helps us avoid confusion. The distinctions between them mean that the three persons exercise different roles and enjoy different relationships with each other. When we speak about the differences in roles or activities, we are talking about the *economic* Trinity. ("Home economics" used to be a subject studied in high school and college. The word *economics* referred to activities, and a home economics student learned how to manage the various jobs and responsibilities of a home.) The Father exercises the role of *Creator,* for we know "in the beginning God created the heavens and the earth" (Genesis 1:1). The Son exercises the role of *Savior,* as the angel announced to the shepherds: "Today in the city of

David was born for you a Savior, who is Christ the Lord" (Luke 2:11). And the Holy Spirit exercises the role of *Sanctifier*—the one who causes Christians and the church to grow—for Paul says we are "sanctified by the Holy Spirit" (Romans 15:16). The three are different because of the different roles they play in the outworking of the divine plan for this world.

More precisely, we should say the Father plays the *primary* role in creation because both the Son as the agent of creation (John 1:3; Colossians 1:16) and the Holy Spirit (Genesis 1:2) also are involved in this activity. Similarly, we should say the Son plays the *primary* role in salvation, though the Father planned it and sent the Son (John 3:16) and the Holy Spirit applies salvation (2 Thessalonians 2:13). Finally, we should say the Holy Spirit plays the *primary* role in sanctification, for both the Father (Hebrews 2:11) and the Son (1 Corinthians 1:2) also are involved in this process of growth. Despite some overlap, however, the three persons are distinguishable by their different activities of creation, salvation, and sanctification.

When we speak about the differences in relationships between the three, we are talking about the *ontological* Trinity. *Ontological* means being, so the ontological Trinity has to do with the being of God in terms of the eternal relationships between the Father, the Son, and the Holy Spirit. Though difficult to understand, a few points can be made about this.

One is that the Father eternally relates to the Son in a paternal relationship. This means that the Father always commands, supervises, and directs the Son, and the Son always submits to him and obeys what he says. This does not mean the Father is superior to the Son and the Son is inferior to the Father. My father (who is a great dad!), though older and much wiser than I am, is not superior to me, his son. And my son (who is a great son!), though younger and less mature than I am, is not in any way inferior to me, his father. Rather, it simply means that the two always relate to each other in a Father-Son relationship. This also means that the Son, who is generated by the Father, is eternally dependent for his existence on the Father. He did not create the Son, but the Father eternally puts the Son in possession of his being. Jesus himself affirms this: "For just as the Father has life in Himself, so also He has granted to the Son to have life in Himself" (John 5:26). In some mysterious way, the Father grants the Son his eternal existence. In other words, an eternal characteristic of the Father in relationship to the Son is *paternity,* and an eternal characteristic of the Son in relationship to the Father is *generation.*

Another point is that the Holy Spirit relates to the Father and the Son as one who proceeds from both of them; thus, an eternal characteristic of the Holy Spirit in relationship to these two is *procession.* The procession of the Holy Spirit means he is eternally dependent for his existence on both the Father and the Son; they did not create him, but he eternally proceeds from them both. We believe this is true because both the Father and the Son sent the Spirit at Pentecost on his mission. Jesus himself spoke of this upcoming event on several occasions during his ministry:

- "The Counselor, the Holy Spirit, whom the Father will *send* in My name" (John 14:26).
- "When the Counselor comes, whom I will *send* to you from the Father—the Spirit of truth who proceeds from the Father" (John 15:26).
- "If I don't go away the Counselor will not come to you. If I go, I will *send* Him to you" (John 16:7 italics mine).

Putting Jesus' teachings on the Holy Spirit together, we see that the Holy Spirit goes out from the Father and is sent by both the Father (who sends him in the name of Jesus) and the Son (who sends him from the Father). Hence, both the Father and the Son sent out the Holy Spirit on Pentecost. This indicates that the two of them have an eternal relationship of directing the Spirit and putting him in possession of his being. According to one of the church's creeds, or statements of faith, the Holy Spirit "proceeds from the Father and the Son."[1]

In summary, the Father, the Son, and the Holy Spirit are three distinct persons in the Trinity. The distinctions are evident in the different roles they exercise—this is the *economic* Trinity. The Father has the primarily role in *creation,* the Son has the primary activity in *salvation,* and the Holy Spirit has the primary function in *sanc-*

tification. The distinctions are also seen in the different relationships they enjoy with each other—this is the ontological Trinity. An eternal characteristic of the Father is *paternity,* an eternal characteristic of the Son is *generation,* and an eternal characteristic of the Holy Spirit is *procession.* These characteristics are revealed in the eternal relationships between the three persons. The Father, the Son, and the Holy Spirit are three distinct persons.

Affirmation 2: Each Person of the Trinity Is Fully God

This second affirmation acknowledges that the Father is fully God, the Son is fully God, and the Holy Spirit is fully God. All that God is, the Father is; all that God is, the Son is; and all that God is, the Holy Spirit is. All of the attributes of God that we have discussed—independence, unchangeableness, eternity, presence everywhere, knowledge of all things, wisdom, power, love, holiness, righteousness or justice, jealousy, truthfulness and faithfulness, sovereignty, mercy and grace, and wrath—apply equally to the Father, the Son, and the Holy Spirit. There is absolutely no difference in these qualities between the three persons of the Trinity. Though distinctions in roles and relationships exist between the three, no differences can be found in terms of deity, attributes, or nature between them.

The Father is fully God. In the case of the Father, it is certainly clear that he is fully God. Everything that we have considered so far is true of him. But what about the Son and the Holy Spirit? Are they fully God just as the Father is?

The Son is fully God. Before becoming the God-man, Jesus Christ, the Son pre-existed as the eternal Word of God. John describes him in this way: "In the beginning was the Word; and the Word was with God, and the Word was God. He was with God in the beginning. All things were created through Him, and apart from Him not one thing was created that has been created" (John 1:1–3).

With opening words just like the start of Genesis—"in the beginning"—John tells us that something—the Word—was already in existence before the world and everything in it was created. This Word was with God, meaning that he was distinct from the Father and enjoyed a personal relationship with him. And this Word was

God, meaning that he was fully divine just as the Father. We later learn that "the Word became flesh and took up residence among us" (John 1:14). The Word who was fully God and who had always existed became the man Jesus Christ. He took on human nature and became fully human like you and me. Jesus Christ is the God-man—he is fully man and fully God.

Occasionally, on Saturday mornings, people from some cults—the Jehovah's Witnesses or Mormons—knock on my door and strike up a conversation about their religion. Inevitably the discussion turns to Jesus Christ, and this passage in John becomes the center of attention. According to my visitors, this passage teaches that the Word is "a god" or "godlike." My visitors show me where their Bible reads, "And the Word was with God, and the Word was a god." They conclude, then, that the Word—Jesus Christ—is not fully God, even though he may be very godlike.

I calmly try to explain to them that their Bible is wrong. Oftentimes this is a bit hard to do because few of them know Greek, the language in which the New Testament was originally written. If we follow the Greek, however, the best translation of John 1:1 is the one we already stated: "In the beginning was the Word; and the Word was with God, and the Word was God."

The Bible affirms that the Word was *God*—not *a god* or *godlike,* but *God.* Every other time the word *God* appears in John's opening chapter, it always refers to the one who is fully and truly God. This is no exception. If further evidence is needed, verse 3 provides it: This Word was the one through whom the world and everything it contains was made. It is absolutely impossible that *a god* or some *godlike being* could create the universe. No, the creation came into existence because God created it. The Word was God, and through him all that exists came into being.

Verse 18 gives even more evidence: "No one has ever seen God. The only Son—the One who is at the Father's side—He has revealed Him" (John 1:18). As we have seen, no one has ever seen God. But there is one who reveals the Father. The Word whom John has described is now called the one and only God. He is not *a god,* and he is not some *godlike being.* Rather, he is the only God who reveals the Father.

This is possible only if Jesus Christ is fully God; otherwise, he could never fully reveal the Father. Because Christ is fully God, however, knowing him means that we know the Father as well, as Jesus tells his friend Philip: "'I am the way, the truth, and the life. No one comes to the Father except through Me. If you know Me, you will also know My Father. From now on you do know Him and have seen Him.' 'Lord,' said Philip, 'show us the Father, and that's enough for us.' Jesus said to him, 'Have I been among you all this time without your knowing Me, Philip? The one who has seen Me has seen the Father. How can you say, "Show us the Father"?'" (John 14:6–9).

Because Jesus Christ is God, to know him is to know the Father. Being truly and fully God, Christ reveals to us the identity of the Father whom no one has ever seen. The writer to the Hebrews makes this same point: "He is the radiance of His glory, the exact expression of His nature" (Hebrews 1:3). The Son, Jesus Christ, is the exact copy of the nature of God the Father. Everything that the Father is—powerful, gracious, merciful, wrathful, sovereign—the Son is also in every way. When we know Jesus Christ, we know the Father, because the Son is fully God.

The Holy Spirit is fully God. We have established that the Father is fully God, and the Son is fully God. The question now becomes, "Is the Holy Spirit fully God?" Overall, less direct evidence exists for this, but the case for the deity of the Spirit can still be made. Because we have established that the Father and the Son are fully God, the passages that link the Holy Spirit with these two imply that the Spirit is fully God like them. So when we read Jesus' instruction about baptism—"baptizing them in the name of the Father and of the Son and of the Holy Spirit" (Matthew 28:19)— and Paul's prayer of blessing—"The grace of the Lord Jesus Christ, and the love of God, and the fellowship of the Holy Spirit be with all of you" (2 Corinthians 13:13)—we rightly conclude that the Holy Spirit is fully God. Any other conclusion—for example, that the Holy Spirit is somewhat less than fully God—would not make any sense.

But there is more. In a frightening story of sin among the early Christians, Ananias and his wife Sapphira sell a piece of property and donate the money earned to the apostles to help other believers in need. This certainly is a generous act, but unfortunately the two make it appear that they give all the proceeds from the sale to the church. In reality, however, they hold on to a part of the money. While there is nothing wrong with that, they sin by making it seem as though they are giving the whole amount. Peter confronts them: "Ananias, why has Satan filled your heart to *lie to the Holy Spirit* and keep back part of the proceeds from the field? Wasn't it yours while you possessed it? And after it was sold, wasn't it at your disposal? Why is it that you planned this thing in your heart? You have not *lied* to men but *to God!*" (Acts 5:3–4, italics mine). Peter exposes the sin of Ananias and Sapphira: Though they tried to deceive people, they ultimately lied to the *Holy Spirit*. That is, they ultimately lied *to God*. Peter parallels lying to the Holy Spirit and lying to God. Indirectly, then, Peter affirms that the Holy Spirit is God.

The Holy Spirit also convincingly demonstrates that he is fully divine by exhibiting the attributes of God. For example, the Holy Spirit is present everywhere, as David acknowledges:

Where can I go from your Spirit?
    Where can I flee from your presence?
If I go up to the heavens, you are there;
    if I make my bed in the depths, you are there.
If I rise on the wings of the dawn,
    if I settle on the far side of the sea,
even there your hand will guide me,
    your right hand will hold me fast. (Psalm 139:7–10)

Also, the Holy Spirit knows everything, "even the deep things of God. For who among men knows the concerns of a man except the spirit of the man that is in him? In the same way, no one knows the concerns of God except the Spirit of God" (1 Corinthians 2:10–11). He knows himself, the other persons of the Trinity, their thoughtful plans and purposes, and all the mysteries of being God. As God himself, the Holy Spirit also acts with divine power. This is nowhere better seen than in the incarnation of the Son of God as Jesus Christ. When Mary asks for an explanation of how she, a virgin, could conceive and give birth to a child, the angel tells her: "The Holy Spirit will come upon you, and the power of the Most High will overshadow you. Therefore the holy child to be born will be called the Son of God. And consider Elizabeth your relative—even she has conceived a son in her old age, and this is the sixth month for her who was called barren. For nothing will be impossible with God" (Luke 1:35–37).

The Holy Spirit exists everywhere, knows all things, and is all-powerful. Because these are attributes that belong to God alone, they demonstrate that the Holy Spirit is indeed fully God.

The Father is fully God. The Son is fully God. The Holy Spirit is fully God. The second affirmation about the three persons of the Trinity—*each of these persons is fully God*—has been demonstrated.

Affirmation 3: There Is Only One God

Up to this point, I have emphasized the distinctions between the three persons of the Trinity. The third affirmation—*there is only one God*—focuses on the unity of these three and emphasizes the oneness of God. This reflects Moses' charge to Israel: "Hear, O Israel: The LORD our God, the LORD is one. Love the LORD your God with all your heart and with all your soul and with all your strength" (Deuteronomy 6:4–5).

The New Testament adds its witness to the uniqueness of God. For example, Paul tells us that "there is one God" (Romans 3:30) and presents Jesus Christ as the mediator between the one God and humanity: "For there is one God and one mediator between God and man, a man, Christ Jesus" (1 Timothy 2:5). Indeed, James explains that the belief that God is one is a very basic idea—for humans as well as demons: "You believe that God is one; you do well. The demons also believe—and they shudder" (James 2:19).

Because of Scripture's constant insistence that there is only one true God, it is hard to imagine how anyone could understand the doctrine of the Trinity as teaching there are three gods. As Isaiah notes:

I am the LORD, and there is no other;
    apart from me there is no God.

I will strengthen you,
> though you have not acknowledged me,
so that from the rising of the sun
> to the place of its setting
men may know there is none besides me.
> I am the LORD, and there is no other. (Isaiah 45:5–6)

Clearly there is only one completely unique and true God. Obviously then, the Father is not one God, while the Son and the Holy Spirit are other Gods. The Bible precludes tritheism—belief in three gods. And the idea that the three are simply united in purpose and in agreement does not go far enough. Rather, the Father, the Son, and the Holy Spirit are one being—one in essence. While eternally existing as three persons, God is one in his essential being.

In summary, I have demonstrated that the doctrine of the Trinity consists of three affirmations:

1. God eternally exists as three distinct persons—the Father, the Son, and the Holy Spirit.
2. Each of these persons is fully God—the Father is fully God, the Son is fully God, and the Holy Spirit is fully God.
3. There is only one God.

Each of these three affirmations is essential to our belief in the Trinity.

Christians and the Triune God

When we as Christians grasp that the one whom we worship is the triune God, our understanding and appreciation of God is greatly enhanced. Because he is Father, Son, and Holy Spirit, our God is completely unlike all other so-called gods. No other religion comes close to understanding God as being triune, or three-in-one. Indeed, other religions specifically deny this truth about God's being. This means that no other religion worships the God who plans, accomplishes, and applies genuine salvation. For no other religion has God the Father who purposes to rescue human beings from sin and condemnation and so sends his one and only Son to do so. No other religion has God the Son who willingly obeys the

Father, leaves his position of glory, humbles himself to become a man, lives among us, and suffers, dies, and rises again as the God-man for the sins of humanity. No other religion has God the Holy Spirit who is sent by the Father and the Son to apply the work of salvation to the lives of individual people like you and me.

Buddhism may encourage people to seek the state of happiness and peace known as nirvana, but it is only by self-discipline and a continual cycle of death and rebirth that they achieve it. At best, many Buddhas exist to help along the way. But no triune God of Father, Son, and Holy Spirit decisively breaks the cycle of suffering and death. Hinduism may encourage people to achieve spiritual perfection so that their souls enter moksha, but it is only by a continuous process of reincarnation related to the law of karma that they arrive there. At best, many gods—especially Brahma, Vishnu, and Shiva (respectively, the creator, preserver, and destroyer of the world)—are involved. But no triune God of Father, Son, and Holy Spirit graciously provides the gift of perfection. Islam may teach people that life is a preparation and test for the next life, and that their good works must outnumber their bad works for them to get into heaven. At best, God is a just judge of peoples' works who gives mercy to those who do good. But no triune God of Father, Son, and Holy Spirit rescues those who can't save themselves—the situation in which all people find themselves. How different our God is—how completely unique he is from the god or gods of all other religions!

The Trinity: A Model of Dynamic Love

Another key for our life is the foundation that the Trinity provides for dynamic, loving relationships in our human community. Because God is love, the Father, the Son, and the Holy Spirit have always loved each other in the community of the Trinity. For this reason, they enjoy an intimate unity among themselves. Jesus reflects on this as he prays to the Father for us: "May they all be one, just as You, Father, are in Me and I am in You. May they also be one in Us, so that the world may believe You sent Me" (John 17:21).

The intimate bond between the persons of the Trinity is eternal and profound, joining the Father, the Son, and the Holy Spirit together not only in purpose and action but in unity of essence. As

Jesus notes, however, there is more. Their dynamic love is not only directed inwardly, to be shared among themselves. Ever since the creation of the world, the three direct their love outwardly, expressing love for us human beings as well. This love creates the bonds that join us together in human community. Certainly we will never experience that bond of unity to the depth and the degree that the Trinity experiences it. Nevertheless, love will bind us together tightly as we live authentically as people created in the image of God.

As we know, *God created us in his image so that we, like a mirror, would reflect him in the world in which we live.* We reflect the dynamic, loving relationships of the community of the Trinity when we develop dynamic, loving relationships in our human community. Patterned after the intimate bonds of love among the Father, the Son, and the Holy Spirit, the love we express and share for one another can be deep and profound. It is a *pursuing love* that won't let go but gets stronger the tougher the situation gets. It is a *gracious love* that forgives when the ones we love hurt us, disappoint us, fail us, sin against us. It is a *reciprocal love* that turns around and forgives us when we hurt, disappoint, fail, and sin against those who love us. It is a *constructive love* that desires the very best for others and so builds them up to become all that God wants them to be. It is a *strong love* that refuses to cripple others by making them dependent on us but points them to complete dependence on God himself. It is a *wise love* that helps others in a discerning way and avoids enabling the weaknesses and sins of others. It is a *just love* that doesn't play favorites but is fair toward everyone. With this kind of love as the foundation of our human community, we as the image bearers of God will together truly reflect him in the world in which we live.

 Imagine being part of a community that is characterized by the kind of love I've just described. It may be that you experience that kind of love in the human community of your family. All human beings long for that kind of family—a constant source of loving support and development. Un-

fortunately, many families today fail and fall apart. So where can those of us who don't experience love in the human community of our family find it? Part of the good news of Jesus Christ is that we can find this love in the new human community of our church. Actually, the church is more than just a human community; as believers in Jesus Christ, we are adopted into the family of God and become his sons and daughters. As members of God's family, we also become members of the new family of the church. We are eternally tied together as brothers and sisters in Christ, and God has designed the church to be the place where we find and experience the authentic love described above.

Paul tells us to "diligently [keep] the unity of the Spirit with the peace that binds us" (Ephesians 4:3). This means that the dynamic love that unites us is first of all a gift of God and not something we need to create; it is already present in the church. Secondly, however, when Paul commands us to "make every effort," he indicates that dynamic, loving relationships require work to develop and strengthen. So how can you do a better job in loving others? What can you do to express a genuine love that is pursuing, gracious, reciprocal, constructive, strong, wise, and just? How can you involve your best friends in working together to better reflect the dynamic, loving relationships between the persons of the Trinity in the new human community of your church?

In the Beginning

CHAPTER 9

As a biology major at a large university, I was completely steeped in the doctrine of evolution. This was no mere theory still in need of further support; rather, it was absolutely certain truth that no one could—or would ever dare—dispute.

As a new believer, I never imagined there could be another explanation for the beginning and development of the universe and the origin of human life. As Christian friends pointed me to books underscoring the problems of evolutionary theory, however, I came to a crisis point in my life: could I abandon everything I had ever believed about the origin and development of this world? And what could I put in its place—the biblical teaching that God was the Creator of all that exists?

One day I got into a debate about evolution with an instructor—in front of a geology class! As I pointed out problems with the theory, he attempted to respond and show there was no real difficulty. Even though outmatched—I was still only a student, and no one else in the room had ever questioned evolution—I felt like I was at least holding my own. Then the teacher turned the tables on me. He boldly and arrogantly pressed this question: "So you really believe in Adam and Eve?"

I felt like time stood still while I considered how I was going to answer. If I denied the historicity of Adam and Eve, I would come into direct conflict with biblical teaching on creation and leave an insurmountable problem for my position. If I affirmed my belief, I would dare to dispute evolution and would become the object of laughter and ridicule.

I stared at the instructor as I slowly and faithfully replied, "Yes, I believe in Adam and Eve."

To this day, I don't recall the response of the teacher and the rest of the class. It really didn't matter. In that moment of decision, I became convinced of something. I never doubted the biblical teaching on creation after that.

Creation Ex Nihilo

"In the beginning God created the heavens and the earth" (Genesis 1:1). With great simplicity and clarity, the Bible opens with an affirmation that God is the Creator of the universe and all that it contains. This has led the church to believe in creation *ex nihilo*— God created everything out of nothing (*ex* means "out of" and *nihilo* means "nothing"). That is, when God created, he did not use already existing material. He did not combine two hydrogen atoms and one atom of oxygen to make H_2O, and he did not take this water and mix it together with dirt to make the solid parts of the world. Before he created the universe, nothing at all existed— except for him.

The Father did this through the creative agency of his Son. John says of the Son: "All things were created through Him, and apart from Him not one thing was created that has been created" (John 1:3). And Paul explains more fully: "Because by Him every-thing was created, in heaven and on earth, the visible and the invisible, whether thrones or dominions or rulers or authorities— all things have been created through Him and for Him" (Colossians 1:16). God did this by powerfully speaking the uni-verse into existence, as Psalm 33 notes:

By the word of the LORD were the heavens made,
their starry host by the breath of his mouth. . . .
For he spoke, and it came to be;
he commanded, and it stood firm. (vv. 6, 9)

Clearly, no human being was present at the creation of the world. We have no eyewitnesses, no photographs, no videos of the creation, so we have no way to confirm that God did this. The Bible emphasizes that we *believe* God created everything—we understand this truth *by faith:* "By faith we understand that the universe was created by the word of God, so that what is seen has been made from things that are not visible" (Hebrews 11:3). By faith we understand that God did not employ previously existing molecules or compounds when he made the universe. Rather, he created the world *ex nihilo* by speaking it and everything it contains into existence by his powerful word through Jesus Christ.

The Process of Creation

The process of creation followed an ordered sequence and took place over the course of six days:

DAY	THE CREATION OF
first	the light (separation of the light from the darkness)
second	the sky (an expanse to separate the water under and above it)
third	the land and the seas; seed-bearing plants and trees
fourth	two great lights (the sun and the moon)
fifth	the living creatures of the sea and the birds
sixth	the living creatures of the land and the wild animals; humanity

As noted in an earlier chapter, everything that preceded the creation of humanity was leading up to that point as the climax of God's creative work. This means the created universe is designed for humanity. Before creating man, God deliberated within himself; the Father, the Son, and the Holy Spirit counseled among themselves: "Let us make man in our image, in our likeness, and let them rule over the fish of the sea and the birds of the air, over the livestock, over all the earth, and over all the creatures that move along the ground" (Genesis 1:26).

Having completed this deliberation, God actualized what he purposed to do. He then blessed his human creation and gave them a command: "So God created man in his own image, in the image of God he created him; male and female he created them. God blessed them and said to them, 'Be fruitful and increase in number; fill the earth and subdue it. Rule over the fish of the sea and the birds of the air and over every living creature that moves on the ground'" (Genesis 1:27–28). This charge to his human creatures reflects a purpose for God's creation of us—to exercise authority over the created order. We have fulfilled this purpose—and continue to do so—in many ways. These include entering into marriages, forming families with children, applying scientific knowledge to plant farmlands and build skyscrapers, and constructing cities with businesses, schools, transportation, and homes. Other ways involve structuring societies with governments and social organizations; expressing creativity in art, music, dance, and sports; furthering communication through cell phones, e-mail, and instant messaging; and enhancing human life by advances in medicine and genetics.

Adam and Eve

God's creation of our first human parents is detailed in the second chapter of Genesis. Whereas the first chapter gives us a global view of creation—the view from the Goodyear blimp—the second chapter focuses on God's creation of the first man and first woman—a film taken with a telephoto lens. The man's creation is recounted simply and in few words; the story of the woman is quite lengthy and detailed.

Adam

As for the man: "The LORD God formed man from the dust of the ground and breathed into his nostrils the breath of life, and man became a living being" (Genesis 2:7). The Hebrew word (the Old Testament was originally written in Hebrew) for man is *adam* and is related to the word for ground—*adamah*. So the first human being is a man from the earth. Taking ground dust and molding it into the form of a human being, God energizes this lifeless sculpture by directly breathing the breath of life into it. Though all living creatures "have the breath of life in them" (Genesis 7:15), only in the case of man does God personally communicate that principle of life. The result of this forming and breathing is the first living human being, the man Adam.

Eve

Much greater detail is given in the biblical story of the woman's creation:

> The LORD God said, "It is not good for the man to be alone. I will make a helper suitable for him." Now the LORD God had formed out of the ground all the beasts of the field and all the birds of the air. He brought them to the man to see what he would name them; and whatever the man called each living creature, that was its name. So the man gave names to all the livestock, the birds of the air and all the beasts of the field. But for Adam no suitable helper was found. So the LORD God caused the man to fall into a deep sleep; and while he was sleeping, he took one of the man's ribs and closed up the place with flesh. Then the LORD God made a woman from the rib he had taken out of the man, and he brought her to the man. The man said, "This is now bone of my bones and flesh of my flesh; she shall be called 'woman,' for she was taken out of man." (Genesis 2:18–23)

Having evaluated the entire creation and declared it "very good" (Genesis 1:31), God now draws attention to something that is not good: the aloneness of the man he has created. No creature exists as Adam's counterpart; no other created being corresponds to him. So God purposes to rectify this situation. He will make a partner for the man. God knows about Adam's aloneness, but to call this to the man's attention, he parades a zoo full of animals in front of him. As Adam sees Mr. and Mrs. Baboon, and Mr. and Mrs. Giraffe, and Mr. and Mrs. Rhinoceros, he is awakened to the fact that there is no Mrs. Human Being—he is alone. Putting him to sleep, God performs surgery on Adam's rib and fashions a woman from it. As God presents his gift to the man, Adam embraces her with great enthusiasm and excitement. He recognizes that she perfectly corresponds to him—she is bone of his bones and flesh of his flesh. No wonder he names her "woman" (in Hebrew, *ishah*) because she was taken from "man" (in Hebrew, *ish*).

In no other ancient book that presents a story of creation do we find an account of the creation of the woman. The focus is always on the creation of the first man, and the creation of the first woman receives no space. How different is our Bible on this point! Certainly this underscores the importance of women, though we know this already from Genesis 1 and its affirmation that both men and women are created in the image of God.

God's creation of humanity as male and female is very significant for us. As we've already seen, this enables us to reflect the dynamic, loving relationships in the Trinity. The biological differences between male and female make it possible for us to procreate—and enjoy the process through the pleasures of sexual intercourse! The differences in expressions of maleness and femaleness add dynamic—and challenging—variety to life.

This means that our gender is a very important part of God's design for us. In our day of gender confusion—sex-change operations, cross-dressing, asexuality, bisexuality—God's creation of us as either male or female gives reason for us to embrace our gender. God did not make a mistake when he created you as a man or a woman. On the contrary, your gender is part of his perfect plan for you in the world in which you live. You are either a man made in God's image or a woman made in God's image—by his unique design!

Can you give thanks to God for the gender that he created you?

"And It Was Very Good"

During the various stages of the process of creation, God looked upon what he had made and "saw that it was good" (Genesis 1:10, 12, 18, 21, 25). Having completed his work of creation with human beings at the apex, God "saw all that he had made, and it was very good" (Genesis 1:31). While pleased with the process, God was especially pleased with the completed product. This was so because the original creation exactly corresponded to God's design for it. Just as he projected it, just as he spoke it powerfully into existence, so the creation existed and flourished. This reminds us that whatever reflects God brings him great pleasure. God does not need us and the creation, and he is fully pleased with himself. But he has designed us and the creation for a purpose, and when we fulfill that purpose and reflect God's design for us, he is pleased.

The creation not only pleases God; it delights us as well. After creating our human parents, God placed them in the Garden of Eden: "And the LORD God made all kinds of trees grow out of the ground—trees that were pleasing to the eye and good for food" (Genesis 2:9). Certainly the creation serves us well—it is "good for food." This reminds us of the goodness of our Creator God, as Paul notes: "[God] did not leave Himself without a witness, since He did good: giving you rain from heaven and fruitful seasons, and satisfying your hearts with food and happiness" (Acts 14:17).

So the creation is useful to us, and it expresses who God is. But creation is more than this—it also is "pleasing to the eye." Like an artist with great creativity and a sense of wonder, God has painted the world with magnificent beauty. Every summer the meadowlands tucked up high in the mountains are ablaze with color as the wildflowers display their purples, oranges, blues, and pinks. Fall in New England brings the annual change of colors as summer greens give way to flaming reds and yellows. The hundreds of shades of browns in the desert, the intense blues of the oceans, the colorful plumage of birds—the world is like a canvas on which God has gone to great lengths to express his artistic genius. He has spared nothing in creating this world, and it is a delight to our senses.

A Tension Point

Christians often feel a conflict with what I have just said and another reality of the creation—this world, and our existence in it, are not going to last forever. It is the tension between *enjoying beauty* and *respecting temporality*. On the one hand, the fact that we are only pilgrims on this earth—Peter calls us "aliens and temporary residents" (1 Peter 2:11)—means that we should live as though we don't live here. We must respect the temporality of our existence in this world. Add to this the fact that the world will one day come to an end, as Peter again explains: "But the day of the Lord will come like a thief; on that day the heavens will pass away with a loud noise, the elements will burn and be dissolved, and the earth and the works on it will be disclosed" (2 Peter 3:10).

We cannot become attached to this world, because it is temporary and will cease to exist. Often this view is combined with a rejection of involvement in environmental issues, social concerns, and human rights causes that could improve the human condition. "Why waste time trying to save something that is inherently doomed to be destroyed?" some argue. Instead, we must respect the temporality of this world's existence.

On the other hand, the creation exudes great beauty. Going far beyond mere usefulness, God has endowed what he created with a magnificent splendor that is pleasing to our senses. Wisdom insists that we appreciate this glorious gift. In Proverbs, wisdom is often personified as a woman who acts, speaks, and gives counsel. In one such personification, wisdom is God's helper during the creation of the universe:

I was the craftsman at God's side.
I was filled with delight day after day,
    rejoicing always in his presence,
rejoicing in his whole world
    and delighting in mankind. (Proverbs 8:30–31)

The response of wisdom to divine creation is that of delight and joy. Wisdom embraces the world and everything that God puts in it, especially his human creatures. Following the counsel of wisdom, therefore, we should enjoy the beauty of creation.

So how do we live with this tension? Should we simply ignore the beauty of the created order? Should we reject living in this world with its God-given pleasures and enjoyments? Should we remain aloof from involvement in causes that focus on human development and improvement? Or should we seek pleasure in the creation? Should we enjoy the world and become attached to something that is passing away? Should we invest our lives in trying to improve a world that is here today and gone tomorrow? Or should we do both—enjoy beauty and respect temporality?

Christians line up on both sides of this tension, so the answer is not an easy one. I would guess that you will wrestle with this conflict all your life—at least, I hope you will! Here's something to think about: Paul expresses it as he addresses people who are well-off in this world (compared with the rest of the world, you and I—no matter what our socioeconomic status is—fall into this group): "Instruct those who are rich in the present age not to be arrogant or to set their hope on the uncertainty of wealth, but on God, who richly provides us with all things to enjoy. Instruct them to do good, to be rich in good works, to be generous, willing to share, storing up for themselves a good foundation for the age to come, so that they may take hold of life that is real" (1 Timothy 6:17–19).

In terms of living in this world, we should avoid several things. We shouldn't be full of pride, arrogantly living as though our abilities and accomplishments are the result of our own self-effort and work. We shouldn't trust in what we have done and what we have accumulated, because those things are uncertain and can disappear very quickly, leaving us with nothing to hold on to. Rather, we should always remember that everything we have is a gift from God, and so our hope should be placed in him. We should use our privileges to do good to others and help those who are less fortunate than we. This obviously includes the poor, the homeless, and the sick. It extends also to friends in desperate family situations and single-parent families who can be helped by neighborhood and school projects like clean-up days, building homes, and distributing school supplies in the fall and toys at Christmas. There is great reward in this, both in terms of a sense of satisfaction and a record of good deeds to please God as he judges us.

Finally—and very important for our discussion—we should enjoy the many good things that God has abundantly given to us. He is no reluctant miser who has to be coerced to hand out a few trinkets here and there. Rather, he "richly provides us with everything for our enjoyment." This strong statement encourages us to view God as a lavish gift-giver who intends for us to enjoy every good thing he provides for us. But what we enjoy here pales in comparison with the pleasures that await us in the age to come. When we go to be with Jesus, then we will "take hold of the life that is truly life." The temporality of human existence on earth demands that we not become overly invested in living in this world. So we should enjoy beauty, and we should respect temporality. We should enjoy life in this world while looking forward to even greater pleasure in the life to come.

Views That Oppose Creation

The doctrine of creation stands in contrast with many different views and philosophies that people hold today.

Materialism

One view that opposes creation is called *materialism*. Though we may immediately think that this view emphasizes the earning and hoarding of cash and possessions—think of materialistic people who always have to have more money, bigger homes, better toys, faster cars—I have a different idea when I speak of materialism. This view holds that all of reality—everything that exists, from planets and stars to human beings and their entire existence—is ultimately material in nature. Even our moral choices, the decisions of our will, our devotion to God and worshiping him, our faith in Jesus Christ, our sense of being guided by the Holy Spirit—everything is the product of matter and natural physical processes. Of course, materialism denies the existence of God. It also denies the existence of the human soul and life after death. Matter and the material world is all there is. What a hopeless way of thinking about our existence! The doctrine of creation insists that materialism is a wrong view of reality.

Pantheism

The doctrine of creation also stands in contrast with *pantheism*. This view (*pan* means "all" and *theos* means "God") holds that God is everything and everything is God. Pantheists equate God with the universe, so some worship the earth, the winds, the trees, water, and fire as being God or gods. Some speak of "mother earth" or "mother nature" as if the physical world and its natural processes are a personal being, making decisions and exercising sovereign control over the course of nature. Some Eastern religions, such as

Buddhism, insist that the goal of human existence is to merge into unity with the universe and eventually become one with God. But it is an error to identify God with his creation, for he is separate from everything that he created. As our holy God, he is exalted above what he made. The doctrine of creation insists that pantheism is a wrong view of reality.

Panentheism

Panentheism is opposed to the doctrine of creation as well. This view (*pan* means "all," *en* means "in," and *theos* means "God") holds that God is in everything. The New Age movement and other cults urge their followers to develop the god who is in them. A key discipline is to fan the flames of the "God-spark" within so as to become more and more like God. Now we Christians agree that God is present everywhere and that we, as his image bearers, are to reflect God in our world by becoming more and more like him. Certainly God is *immanent,* intimately associated with his creation: he is "'Immanuel'—which means, 'God with us'" (Matthew 1:23 NIV)! But Christianity includes a major point of difference from panentheism: God is not only immanent; he is also *transcendent.* That is, God cannot be contained in everything that exists. His existence is not limited to what exists now. He is far greater than the universe and indeed rules over it. The doctrine of creation insists that panentheism is a wrong view of reality.

Dualism

Another view that conflicts with the doctrine of creation is *dualism.* This view (*dual* means "composed of two") holds that two forces—God and the universe—have eternally existed and are locked in mortal combat with each other. In the numerous installments of *Star Wars,* the two sides of the "Force"—the good side and the dark side—are a form of dualism. The philosopher Plato believed that the human spirit is inherently good and the material body is inherently evil. Some Christians treat Satan and his power as being almost on equal footing with God and his grace. Good versus evil, the spirit versus the body, God versus Satan—these are common examples of dualism. In each type of dualism, something exists that is as ultimate as God himself. Of course dualism denies that God is the only sovereign Lord who rules over all that exists. Dualism also places the future in jeopardy, for if dualism were true, it could be the case that evil will ultimately triumph over God and his design for the universe. Finally, dualism is critical of creation, viewing it as inherently bad and thus something that we should reject. The apostle Paul, however, reminds us of the goodness of this world because it was created by God: "For everything created by God is good, and nothing should be rejected if it is received with thanksgiving" (1 Timothy 4:4). The doctrine of creation insists that dualism is a wrong view of reality.

Evolution

The doctrine of creation also stands in contrast with several common scientific theories about the beginning and development of the universe and the origin of human life. The most widespread one is *evolution*. This view maintains that through a process of gradual change, beginning with nonliving matter, all that exists has come into existence and developed without God. This process occurred over the course of billions of years and involved random mutations (accidental changes in the genetic makeup of living beings), natural selection (the favoring of creatures best suited for survival in their environment), and speciation (the development of new species through wholesale, rapid change). God is not a factor in this process, for evolution occurs by completely random, natural, and material changes.

Any completely evolutionary explanation of the origin and development of the universe must be rejected by Christians. The most important reason for this is the clear Scriptural teaching that God did indeed create the world and all that is in it. Another reason is the growing number of problems with evolutionary theory, difficulties pointed out by both Christians and nonbelieving scientists. For example, Michael Behe points out the amazing complexity of even the simplest living organisms. The idea that this complexity was built up gradually from simpler parts and systems doesn't make any sense, because before those parts and systems come together and function as a whole, they are meaningless on their own. Behe illustrates this by analyzing a simple mousetrap. The various parts—platform, spring, catch, holding bar, hammer—are useless apart from one another, so they would never gradually join together to form a mousetrap over time. The irreducible complexity of this simple machine demands that the various parts exist all together as a mousetrap, and it does not leave room for a gradual development of those parts into the whole. When this principle of irreducible complexity is applied to even the simplest living organisms—which are far more complex than a mousetrap—the theory of evolutionary development is shown to be full of problems.[1] The doctrine of creation, together with a growing number of difficulties with the theory of evolution, insists that evolution is a wrong view of creation and its origin and development.

Theistic Evolution

A second view also embraces evolution but is differentiated from the first view by allowing for God in the process; thus, it is called *theistic evolution*. According to this view, God used evolutionary processes to produce most of what we see in the world. At times, however, God intervened in the process. He did so at the beginning of the universe to create the original matter from which everything else would take shape. He intervened in the evolutionary process to introduce the simplest life-forms from which all organic matter or living things would eventually arise. He stepped into the evolutionary development of hominids—precursors to *homo sapiens*—to produce human beings. Apart from these few interventions, however, God normally used the process of evolution to develop the world as we now know it.

Theistic evolution's explanation of the origin and development of the universe must also be rejected by Christians. The most important reason for this is its conflict with the biblical picture of God's design for and control over the creation. Reading the account of creation in Genesis, we note God's purposeful fashioning of light, sky, land, sea, plants and trees, sea creatures and birds, land creatures and wild animals—they are preparatory for his ultimate creative thrust, which is the creation of human beings in his image. This Master-planned project stands in stark contrast with the randomness principle of evolution. This principle insists that mutations, or changes to the genetic makeup of living organisms, occur with complete randomness; no purposefulness is allowed. If the commonly held idea that most mutations are harmful, not beneficial, is correct, then theistic evolution must believe that purely accidental and mostly damaging changes were the driving force behind the development of the universe. This ugly, destructive model is at complete odds with the biblical model of creation being carried out with divine wisdom and evoking delight and joy. Another reason for rejecting theistic evolution is the many problems with evolutionary theory, as discussed above. The doctrine of creation, together with a growing number of difficulties with the theory of evolution, insists that theistic evolution is a wrong view of creation and its origin and development.

Creationism

Rejecting both evolution and theistic evolution as explanations for the origin and development of the universe, most Christians are united on the following points:

- God created the universe and all that it contains, and he created it *ex nihilo,* or out of nothing, by speaking the world into existence by his powerful word through Jesus Christ.
- The process of creation followed an ordered sequence leading up to the creation of humanity as the climax of God's creative work.
- This special creation of human beings involved a divine deliberation by the Father, the Son, and the Holy Spirit, followed by the actualization of their plan—the creation of Adam and Eve in the image of God.
- God was pleased with his finished product, and the creation also pleases us and expresses what God is like.

While general agreement exists on these points, Christians are divided on several other issues about the doctrine of creation. In fact, most Christians fall into one of two camps—*young earth creationism* and *progressive* (or *old earth*) *creationism.* A number of points separate these diverse perspectives.

Young Earth Creationism

On the one hand, *young earth creationism* believes that God's creative work was accomplished during a six-day period of time. That is, the term *day* used in Genesis 1 refers to a twenty-four-hour period, as indicated by the expression "and there was evening, and there was morning—the first [or second, or third, or fourth, or fifth, or sixth] day" (Genesis 1:5, 8, 13, 19, 23, 25). This is confirmed by the fourth commandment, in which God's six-day creation followed by a seventh day of rest—"For in six days the LORD made the heavens and the earth, the sea, and all that is in them, but he rested on the seventh day" (Exodus 20:11)—becomes the pattern for human work and rest. According to young earth creationism, the actual age of the earth is quite young; it is perhaps only tens of thousands of years old or less. Alleged scientific evidence to the contrary—demonstrations that the earth's age is in the billions of years—is based on faulty measurements and wrong presuppositions.

Progressive Creationism

On the other hand, *progressive* (or *old earth*) *creationism* believes that God's creative work was done over the course of a long period of time. The earth is far older than tens of thousands of years, as much reliable scientific evidence demonstrates; indeed, it is many billions of years old. But this does not mean that God employed evolution to establish the world; rather, his creation took place progressively over a long period of time. He established and developed an initial environment; when that was settled, he created a higher level. Having established and developed that second level, he added a third level, and so on. According to some progressive creationists, the term *day* in Genesis 1 actually refers to a long span of time. For example, God took tens of millions or hundreds of millions of years in creating, developing, and diversifying the many seed-bearing plants and fruit trees on the "third day" (Genesis 1:11–13). Other progressive creationists believe that the actual twenty-four-hour "days" in Genesis 1 are separated by long ages of time. According to this view, God did indeed create the seed-bearing plants and fruit trees on the "third day," but those plants and trees underwent development and diversification over the course of tens of millions or hundreds of millions of years before God embarked on his next creative act on the fourth day.

For most of its existence, the church has believed that God created the universe and everything in it in a six-day period of time only several thousands of years ago. Indeed, in the seventeenth century, James Ussher attempted to calculate the exact time of the creation and placed it in the year 4004 B.C. Scientific discoveries in the past century or so urge us to reevaluate these proposals. Just how old the earth is—tens of thousands of years old at the most, according to young earth creationism, or billions of years old at the least, according to old earth creationism—is a point that divides Christians. One key element leading to the diversity of views is the correlation of scientific evidence with biblical teaching. Another key element leading to differences is the interpretation of Genesis 1 and other biblical passages.

PAUSE TIME— Though it is beyond the scope of this book to enter into this debate, I urge you to do research on it. Many excellent books are available in libraries and bookstores.

Creation Glorifies God

God's creation of the universe and all that it contains glorifies him and leads to great praise. Specifically, the creation shows forth God's power, wisdom, and knowledge, as Jeremiah affirms:

God made the earth by his power;
>   he founded the world by his wisdom
>   and stretched out the heavens by his understanding.
(Jeremiah 10:12)

Furthermore, the creation demonstrates the sovereignty of God, as this song of praise echoes:

>   Our Lord and God,
>   You are worthy to receive
>   glory and honor and power,

because You have created all things,
and because of Your will
they exist and were created. (Revelation 4:11)

God sovereignly willed to create the world that, by supplying the needs of people everywhere, displays his goodness as well: "[God] did not leave Himself without a witness, since He did good: giving you rain from heaven and fruitful seasons, and satisfying your hearts with food and happiness" (Acts 14:17).

Power, wisdom, knowledge, sovereignty, goodness—these and other attributes of God are reflected in the creation. As we contemplate the wonders of the created world, praise wells up within us. No wonder we find many songs of praise to God for his creation in Scripture! For example: "Blessed be your glorious name, and may it be exalted above all blessing and praise. You alone are the LORD. You made the heavens, even the highest heavens, and all their starry host, the earth and all that is on it, the seas and all that is in them. You give life to everything, and the multitudes of heaven worship you" (Nehemiah 9:5–6).

Be sure to worship God with great praise for his mighty work of creation!

Well Planned from Beginning to End

CHAPTER 10

While attending a missions conference, my wife and I were challenged with some decisions about our lifestyle that could result in us being more committed to furthering the cause of Jesus Christ worldwide. One of those decisions involved our spending patterns. We were challenged with this: whenever we purchase a luxury item—something that is not essential—give the same amount to a missionary or missions project. The challenge came with this intriguing promise: God would honor our giving and bless us, for Jesus himself said, "Give, and it will be given to you; a good measure, pressed down, shaken together, and running over will be poured into your lap. For with the measure that you use, it will be measured back to you" (Luke 6:38).

Even if Jesus did make this promise, accepting this challenge seemed quite difficult to us at first because it would mean two things. First, it would force us to think very carefully about whether we really wanted the luxury item. Second, it would cost us double the amount of money we would spend on any nonessential purchase. Despite these reservations, and counting on the promise of Jesus, we decided to go ahead and take up the challenge.

Because we were newly married, a gift that we decided to buy for each other and for our first home was a rocking chair. As we drove away from the store with our new piece of furniture, we looked at each other and agreed that the challenge applied to this purchase. When we got home we wrote out a check for $159.41

and sent it off to help a missionary friend. A deep sense of satisfaction settled over us, and we were pleased that we were already making a greater impact for Christ than we previously had made.

Not long afterward, we received an encouraging letter from a former college roommate of mine. He spoke highly of the influence we had exercised in his life, and he expressed his desire to thank us concretely. Because he had just won salesman of the month with his company, he was sending us his monetary award—$125. We were very encouraged, to say the least! Several days later we received a letter from our insurance company. Because we had moved from one location to another, our auto insurance rate had gone down, so the company was sending us a cash rebate. The check nearly fell out of our hands when we looked at the amount— $34.41. These two completely unexpected checks totaled up to $159.41—the exact same amount that we had spent on our rocking chair and in turn had given to missions!

Now, some people hearing this story would draw the conclusion that this chain of events was simply and completely a matter of coincidence. The exact correspondence of what we gave away and the $159.41 we received was nothing more than a chance occurrence. Obviously, my wife and I—and I hope you too—drew a different conclusion based on what we know of God. We detected his mighty hand behind these events, orchestrating this "conspiracy of circumstances" to bless us, fulfill the promise of Jesus, and solidify our commitment to world missions. God has created the world with a purpose, and he is continually at work to bring about his plan and accomplish his will in all things. Our story is but one example of this marvelous truth.

God's Providence

Mere coincidence or divine providence? Do the circumstances of our lives happen accidentally, randomly, by chance? Or do the events that occur and the people who come and go in our lives enact a well-planned drama that fulfills the purpose of God? Many people believe that life is nothing more than coincidence. They have no conception, or have lost the sense, that a divine purpose lies embedded in the created order and becomes expressed through everything that takes place. The church has always believed differently, however, holding to a worldview of divine providence. God's *providence* is his continual, personal, and intimate involvement with everything that he has created to bring about his good pleasure and eternal plan. According to our worldview, chance, coincidence, accidents, and random happenings are ruled out. Rather, all that comes to pass is the outworking of the comprehensive, sovereign plan of our mighty God.

In one sentence, the apostle Paul sums up the providence of God: "In Him we were also made His inheritance, predestined according to the purpose of the One who works out everything in agreement with the decision of His will" (Ephesians 1:11).

God has a plan for us Christians, a plan that was conceived before we even existed. According to this plan, God has predestined us—chosen us to become his sons and daughters through Jesus Christ. He has rescued us from sin and eternal separation from him because he is a gracious and loving God. We are Christians because of God's gracious choice of us!

But there is much more. God's predestination of us to become believers is only part of the story of his awesome and comprehensive work in the world. Indeed, God has purposed and now works *all* things in accordance with his will. Everything that comes to pass—the creation of the universe, human history, the life and death of Jesus, our eternal destiny of heaven or hell, the future—is the outworking of what God has planned for this world and our existence in it.

Scripture stays away from abstract descriptions of God's providence. Rather, God's plan and its effective outworking is presented as an essential part of the biblical worldview through narratives. For example, Joseph is the favorite son of Jacob, but he infuriates his brothers by telling them about a dream in which he, the youngest of all, becomes the ruler of them all. To get back at him, his brothers sell Joseph into slavery while making it appear that a wild animal has devoured him. Achieving great success in Egypt, the country to which he is sent as a slave, Joseph rises to a position of prominence, second in command to Pharaoh. He is particularly diligent in storing up food for future times of famine.

Because of his wise supervision, Joseph saves the people of Egypt from starvation. Hearing that there is adequate food there, Joseph's brothers go to buy grain in Egypt from—who else—Joseph, but they have no idea who he is. Realizing that his dream has come true—he is indeed in a position to rule over his brothers—Joseph reveals himself to his brothers, who are terrified that he might exact revenge and punish them for their treacherous plot against him: "But Joseph said to them, 'Don't be afraid. Am I in the place of God? You intended to harm me, but God intended it for good to accomplish what is now being done, the saving of many lives'" (Genesis 50:19–20). Though his brothers' schemes were intended to cause him harm, Joseph looks behind their evil acts to see God's hand of providence at work to move him into a position to bring about good. What Joseph's brothers intended for evil, God worked for good. Their "conspiracy of circumstances" accomplishes his plan.

The events leading up to and ending in the death of Jesus also demonstrate the providence of God. Peter describes this in one of his sermons: "Jesus the Nazarene was a man approved to you by God with miracles, wonders, and signs that God did among you through Him, just as you yourselves know. Though He was delivered up according to God's determined plan and foreknowledge, you used lawless people to nail Him to a cross and kill Him" (Acts 2:22–23).

The disciples offer praise for the fulfillment of the divine plan as they pray to God: "Herod and Pontius Pilate, with the Gentiles and the peoples of Israel, assembled together against Your holy Servant Jesus, whom You anointed, to do whatever Your hand and Your plan had predestined to take place" (Acts 4:27–28).

God's set purpose and will was that Jesus would suffer death at the hands of wicked people. The crucifixion itself—down to the specific major players of Herod, Pontius Pilate, the Roman soldiers, and the Jews—was the exact outworking of God's plan, the precise fulfillment of his wise strategy to save human beings from sin and destruction. The "conspiracy of circumstances" enacted God's providential purpose for our salvation.

God's Decree

By now, this point is certain and clear: God has a purpose for the world that he created, and he is at work in everything to actualize this plan, which is called his decree. God's *decree* is his eternal plan by which he determined to bring about everything that happens for his great glory. Before creating the world—we might say from eternity past—God purposed to do what he would do. That means his plan is not being constructed as events occur and time rolls on. What we see taking place in our world is the outworking of God's decree, but his plan has always been set in place. Indeed, God's decree guarantees that everything that comes to pass takes place exactly as he purposed. His decree is 100 percent effective, as the Bible assures us. Psalm 33 points us back to the effectiveness of God in creating the world as an assurance of the effectiveness of his decree:

[God] spoke, and it came to be;

he commanded, and it stood firm . . .

The plans of the LORD stand firm forever,

the purposes of his heart through all generations.

(vv. 9, 11)

God himself assures us that his plan will be accomplished:

Surely, as I have planned, so it will be,

and as I have purposed, so it will stand . . .

This is the plan determined for the whole world;

this is the hand stretched out over all nations.

For the LORD Almighty has purposed, and who can thwart him?

His hand is stretched out, and who can turn it back?

(Isaiah 14:24, 26–27)

He adds:

My purpose will stand,

and I will do all that I please . . .

What I have said, that will I bring about;

what I have planned, that will I do. (Isaiah 46:10–11)

We can have complete confidence that God is in control of this world and is carrying out his decree.

God's Decree in Our Lives

Amazingly, God's decree encompasses everything—absolutely everything! It includes the events and circumstances of our lives; indeed, each and every day of life has been established and designed by God, as David notes:

I praise you because I am fearfully and wonderfully made;
> your works are wonderful,
> I know that full well. . . .
All the days ordained for me
> were written in your book
> before one of them came to be. (Psalm 139:14, 16)

The story of our lives was determined before we were even born. Certainly, this includes the good things that we do as believers, as Paul affirms: "We are His making, created in Christ Jesus for good works, which God prepared ahead of time so that we should walk in them" (Ephesians 2:10). As we engage in helping others, sharing the good news of Jesus, trusting and obeying God, we should have a sense that we are fulfilling God's eternal plan for us to do these good works. Even if they don't realize it, unbelievers who do good for others are also fulfilling God's decree. An example of this is Cyrus, a pagan king who decided to help the people of God to return to the land of Israel after seventy years in exile:

I am the LORD, . . . who says of Cyrus, "He is my shepherd
> and will accomplish all that I please;
> he will say of Jerusalem, 'Let it be rebuilt,'
> and of the temple, 'Let its foundations be laid.'"
(Isaiah 44:24, 28)

In helping the Israelites, Cyrus was enacting God's decree—whether Cyrus knew it or not.

God's plan for our lives also includes our plans—at least some of them: "Many are the plans in a man's heart, but it is the LORD's purpose that prevails" (Proverbs 19:21). Certainly as we purpose to do good for others, God helps us to carry out our plan—which is also part of his plan. But what about evil desires and wrong intentions—how do they fit in with God's decree? At this point, our discussion takes a strange twist, for God's plan encompasses even the evil plans and actions of people. We have already seen this both with Joseph and with Jesus. Though his brothers plotted evil against him, Joseph recognized that their sinful actions were part of God's ultimate plan to bring about good. And though a cast of characters conspired together to crucify Jesus, we know that his death was the fulfillment of God's eternal purpose to accomplish our salvation. No wonder the proverb says: "The LORD works out everything for his own ends—even the wicked for a day of disaster" (Proverbs 16:4).

PAUSE TIME— Watch out! This truth should never be abused so as to become an excuse for us to do evil. We should never think: "Well, even if I do wrong, my sin is part of God's decree. So I'll go ahead and do evil, which will be good because it accomplishes his eternal plan." The absurdity of this thinking is clear, as Paul emphasizes: "How can we who died to sin still live in it?" (Romans 6:2). Nor should we reason: "God allows evil and then uses it to bring about good. Therefore I can allow evil to take place and then turn it around for good." While we are encouraged to imitate God in many ways, this is not one of them. At no point in Scripture are we ever told to sin or to encourage sin as a means to bring about good. Remember: God is all-knowing and all-powerful; we are not. We are not in a position to be able to do what God is able to do. He is able to work out everything in conformity with his decree; we are not.

God's Decree in the World

God's decree extends beyond our individual lives to matters of national and international importance. "[God] makes nations great, and destroys them; he enlarges nations, and disperses them" (Job 12:23). As Daniel acknowledges: "[God] changes times and seasons; he sets up kings and deposes them" (Daniel 2:21). He adds: "The Most High is sovereign over the kingdoms of men and gives them to anyone he wishes" (Daniel 4:25). Despite their air of invincibility and demonstrations of power, even the mightiest leaders in this world pale in comparison with our all-powerful God. He accomplishes his decree through them, fulfilling his plan through their decisions and actions. Proverbs 21:1 reminds us that "the king's heart is in the hand of the LORD; he directs it like a watercourse wherever he pleases."

God's Decree in "Random" Events

Each and every day of our lives, the good actions and intentions of people, the evil deeds and plans of people, national and international matters—all are included in God's decree. But there is more. God's decree encompasses "chance" events, as Proverbs 16:33 teaches: "The lot is cast into the lap, but its every decision is from the LORD."

The casting of lots is similar to rolling dice or picking straws. For example, suppose a teacher needs a "volunteer" for a class assignment. She puts the names of every student into a bag and then draws the "lucky" winner. It is a completely "random" event—at least to our way of thinking. But it is not so according to God's decree, for even random, chance events are part of his will.

God's Decree in the Mundane

God's plan even extends to the most mundane, or ordinary, events of life—including dead birds and bad-hair days. Jesus draws our attention to this: "Aren't two sparrows sold for a penny? Yet not one of them falls to the ground without your Father's consent. But even the hairs of your head have all been counted" (Matthew 10:29–30). Jesus means that sparrows are virtually worthless—poor people buy two for a penny. Despite this seeming worthlessness, however, God has the life of each and every bird in mind. We couldn't care less whether a sparrow lives or dies, but what happens to it is part of God's will. He has even counted the hairs on our heads. Such apparently trivial matters like dice throwing, bird survival, and hair numbering enter into the decree of God. The point is this: If God's purpose extends to even these minute, unimportant details, how much more does his providence include the big things of our lives? And that brings us back to Paul's teaching about "the purpose of the One who works out everything in agreement with the decision of His will" (Ephesians 1:11). God's decree is all-encompassing.

Human Freedom and Responsibility

If God is in control of everything, then a major objection arises: What about human freedom and responsibility? If God is sovereignly working out his all-encompassing decree, aren't we human beings reduced to robots—machines without minds, feelings, and self-determining wills, programmed to do God's bidding? Aren't we stripped of our humanness, becoming mere puppets manipulated one way or another so as to enact the script written by God? And if we are like this, how can we be considered responsible human beings who are held accountable for our actions and intentions? Indeed, how could God ever find fault with us if, even when we sin and do evil, we still accomplish his plan for the world?

The church has always wrestled with this very important issue. At times, it has gone to one extreme or the other. Some Christians overly emphasize the sovereignty of God and his decree, almost to the point of embracing *fatalism*. Fatalism is the worldview that everything that exists and happens exists and happens necessarily—things are such that they could not be any other way. Some even believe that God himself was constrained to plan things as he did. Obviously, this perspective on God and his decree rules out all human freedom. For this reason, it is in error. Other Christians, going to the opposite extreme, overly emphasize human freedom and make God dependent on human decisions and actions. Some go so far as to embrace *openness theism*. Openness theism is the worldview that God cannot have a plan for human beings that will be effectively realized because he cannot know what we will decide and do until we make our decision and act. Obviously, this perspective seriously compromises divine sovereignty and dismisses the notion of an effective divine decree. For this reason, it is in error. Both fatalism and openness theism must be rejected by Christians.

Rather than embracing one or the other extreme on this issue, what if we accept two truths and attempt to hold them together, even if they appear to be in tension? This worldview is called *compatibilism*. Compatibilism believes that the following two truths can and should be held together; that is, they are compatible:

1. God is absolutely sovereign. He effectively works out his eternal plan by which he determined to bring about everything that happens for his great glory. But this reality never functions in such a way that human freedom and responsibility is minimized or destroyed.

2. Human beings are responsible and significantly free creatures. They choose, rebel, obey, defy, trust, do good, and commit sin, and they are accountable to God for everything they do. But this reality never functions in such a way that God becomes dependent on human decisions and actions.[1]

According to compatibilism, God sovereignly works out his eternal plan through the decisions and actions of responsible, free human beings. *How* this can be the case is a mystery because on the surface it appears that God's predetermined plan rules out freedom and responsibility, or human freedom and responsibility make it impossible for God to effectively bring about his decree. Just because it is a mystery, however, doesn't mean it is wrong or not true.

In fact, we have already seen several biblical examples of compatibilism. One is the story of Joseph; the other is the drama of Jesus' crucifixion. Let's focus on this second example. Did our sovereign God purpose from all eternity to accomplish our salvation through the death of his Son? Yes, he did. Did Herod, Pontius Pilate, the Roman soldiers, and the religious leaders of Israel conspire against Jesus, plotting and then carrying out their strategy to crucify him? Yes, they did. Did the sovereignty of God in enacting his eternal plan minimize or destroy the freedom and responsibility of those involved in the death of Jesus? No, it did not. Herod would hear of no other king, so he wanted to do away with the one called "the king of the Jews." Pontius Pilate was a weakling who, consistent with his character, gave in to the crowd's wishes to release Barabbas and crucify Jesus. The Roman soldiers were callused executioners who were well trained in the gruesome task of crucifixion. The religious leaders felt threatened by this untrained yet popular and miracle-working Jesus, whom they had tried to kill several times before. Both as individuals and together as major players in this conspiracy, they made their own decisions and carried out their evil actions, eventually crucifying Jesus. Did their freedom and responsibility make God dependent on their decisions and actions? No, it did not. On the contrary, what they did perfectly fulfilled God's sovereign plan for our salvation.

Compatibilism can also be seen in our own experience of salvation. The Bible is clear that one aspect of God's decree is his decision that we would become followers of Jesus Christ. This is the first part of one of the key passages for our discussion: "In Him we were also made His inheritance, predestined according to the purpose of the One who works out everything in agreement with the decision of His will" (Ephesians 1:11). In the same passage, Paul says: "[God] chose us in Him, before the foundation of the world, to be holy and blameless in His sight. In love He predestined us to be adopted through Jesus Christ for Himself, according to His favor and will" (Ephesians 1:4–5).

Before the creation of the world God graciously decided to bring us into his family as adopted sons and daughters. As we listened to the gospel, God was at work to draw us to himself, for Jesus tells us that "no one can come to Me unless the Father who sent Me draws him" (John 6:44). As we heard the good news, the Holy Spirit impressed upon us the error of our sin, the hopelessness of our self-righteousness, and the futility of our worldly judgment (John 16:8–11). People prayed for us, loved us, and communicated the message of Jesus Christ to us. Our sovereign God was graciously and effectively working out this eternal plan for our salvation through this "conspiracy of circumstances." As we realized our dreadful situation, as we understood what we needed to do to embrace God's offer of salvation, we turned from our sin and placed our faith in Jesus Christ. This was in accordance with our own desires and will, and we responsibly and freely repented and believed, resulting in the fulfillment of God's sovereign decree.

Paul describes this compatibilism in our salvation: "We must always thank God for you, brothers loved by the Lord, because from the beginning God has chosen you for salvation through sanctification by the Spirit and through belief in the truth. He called you to this through our gospel, so that you might obtain the glory of our Lord Jesus Christ" (2 Thessalonians 2:13–14). In his sovereignty and in accordance with his eternal decree, God chose us and called us for salvation through Jesus Christ, and the Holy Spirit worked to bring this about. At the same time, in accordance with our own desires and will, we responsibly and freely believed in the truth, the message of Jesus Christ as unfolded in the gospel. Both truths—God's sovereignty and decree, and human responsibility and freedom—are compatible. We know this for sure because our salvation demonstrates them to be so.

This compatibilistic worldview encourages us to be more bold and faithful in prayer and evangelism. Some believe that because God "works out everything in agreement with the decision of His will" (Ephesians 1:11), prayer and evangelism serve no purpose. They think that God's plan will be accomplished no matter if we pray and share the good news or not. But we have seen that God not only designs the big things; his decree also encompasses the minutest details. This means that God plans the ends as well as the means. He not only graciously chooses people for salvation, he also designs all the steps leading up to and resulting in their salvation. One of those means is the prayers of Christians for those who don't yet know Christ. Another one of those means is Christians sharing the gospel so that those who don't yet know Christ can believe in him. We become significant players in God's work in the world in which we live by faithfully praying for our friends and boldly communicating the good news to them.

Compatibilism affirms that God sovereignly works out his eternal plan through the decisions and actions of responsible, free human beings. As I carefully and thoughtfully consider this worldview, it seems to be consistent with what the Bible reveals about

God and his work in the world through us human beings. It also helps me make sense of what I experience of God and his ways. Despite this, I still find that a great deal of God's actions in my life and the lives of others remains a deep mystery. For example, how does it happen that we who are far from God find ourselves desiring to know him personally? Before I became a Christian, I was largely indifferent toward God. Sure, I believed in his existence, I showed up for church on Sundays, and I tried to be moral and do good—but that was the extent of my involvement with him. How did I move from indifference to acceptance, and from acceptance to deep commitment, and from deep commitment to dedication of my entire life to him? Of course, this is by God's gracious choice and work in my life, yet I also decide and act as a responsible, free human being. And what about my friends who overtly rebelled against God before coming face-to-face with the gospel and embracing Jesus Christ? How did they move from enemies to lovers of God, and do so as responsible, free human beings? I know the change takes place. I see the good results in my life and in the lives of my friends. I believe it is because of the grace of God and his powerful work. I know we decide and act as responsible, free human beings. Yet I don't understand how it all works out. It is such a mystery!

Jesus said this himself when talking to Nicodemus about his need to be born again: "Do not be amazed that I told you that you must be born again. The wind blows where it pleases, and you hear its sound, but you don't know where it comes from or where it is going. So it is with everyone born of the Spirit" (John 3:7–8). I have never seen the wind. I hear it blowing, even howling at times. I see it blow leaves and even bow down trees, but I have never seen the wind itself. Similarly, I have never seen God the Holy Spirit. I hear the stories of his impact, even his radical transformation of friends' lives. I see the change he brings about in individuals and families—none greater than moving indifferent and rebellious people to bow down and worship him. But I have never seen God himself in his mysterious undertakings. Yet I believe he works sovereignly to accomplish his eternal plan through the decisions and actions of free, responsible human beings. Without constraining us, without forcing us to go against our own nature and desires, God works mysteriously in us "for His good purpose" (Philippians 2:13). I am very thankful that God does this, even if I don't understand the mystery of how he works.

PAUSE TIME— Personalizing providence: God is continually, personally, and intimately involved in your life to bring about his good pleasure and eternal plan. You are an absolutely unique individual—a "one-of-a-kind" person, unlike anyone who has ever existed or will exist in the future. God himself specially designed you, creating you with the characteristics that make you who you are. These include your gender, race (or ethnicity), body type, height and weight, appearance, your abilities in sports and weaknesses in music and math (or vise versa), and your handicaps and disabilities. His unique design includes the family into which you were born, where you live, your school, the courses and extracurricular activities in which you participate, and the friendships you enjoy. As a believer in Jesus Christ, God graciously chose you by design to be his child and has placed you into the new community of your church. His unique design extends into the future to encompass your future career, your future husband or wife or singleness, whether you will be rich or poor, famous or anonymous, how you will live—even how and when you will die.

This unique design of all you are and will be is part of God's wise and sovereign plan for everything—a plan that is being effectively worked out. This by no means minimizes or destroys your responsibility to cooperate with God—as the unique person he made you—in the accomplishment of his will. Therefore, make the contribution you and only you can make. Work hard. Trust and obey God. Pray and tell others about Jesus Christ. Flee from sin. Worship God.

Not mere coincidence, but divine providence.

The Evil Case against God

CHAPTER 11

Earlier, I told you about a crazy outing that my pastor Bruce and I had one day on Hawthorne Street, a bohemian neighborhood between the school where I teach and our church. (Remember, we video-interviewed people by asking them this question: "If you could ask God any question, what would you ask him?" The second-most popular response was this: "What is the purpose for my life?" Now I want to tell you about the most popular answer.) As we walked by Noah's Bagels, Bruce stopped dead in his tracks and told me to look in. Three goths were inside the shop eating, and they looked like prime candidates for our film. The tall guy had long, flaming red hair, the short guy had a jet black buzz cut, and the woman sported a zebra-striped mohawk. Of course, they were dressed all in black with dog collars, spikes, and lots of piercings and tattoos.

We approached them, explained our video project, and asked if we could sit down and interview them. The tall guy scoffed at us, complaining, "You just want to interview us because we're freaks!" Bruce didn't miss a beat: "You know, we have interviewed rich people and poor people, working people and homeless people, skinheads and hippies, atheists and believers—we've talked with all types. But we haven't interviewed any freaks yet." That's all they needed to hear—they welcomed us to join them at their table.

It wasn't long before the conversation turned to the question they would ask of God: "If you exist, God, why is there so much pain, suffering, and evil in the world?" For the woman, her suffering came in the form of rejection by just about everyone. She is rejected because of being a woman, because she holds strong opinions, and because she chooses to live a gothic lifestyle—and people judge her simply by the way she looks and dresses. The short guy felt cheated by several tragedies in his life. The tall guy seethed hatred toward us as Christians because his brother—who had become a born-again Christian a few years earlier—told him he was going to hell. He embraced Buddhism instead, and believed that life consists of numerous cycles of pain and suffering that one could only hope would eventually lead to peace in nirvana. "Why does life need to be so hard, so full of evil and heartache?" he asked. "Couldn't God do something about this, if he is truly good and powerful?" he pleaded. He concluded: "I don't believe God exists because there is far too much pain and suffering in this world."

"God, if you exist, why is there pain and suffering? If you are completely good and all powerful, then why don't you do something about the evil in this world?" This turned out to be the most popular question we encountered in our interviews.

The Problem of Evil

The problem of evil is the most perplexing issue that people face in relationship to rejecting or trusting in God. For some, it is the reason they doubt or even deny the existence of God. For others, the problem of evil is at the core of their intense hatred and seething anger toward God. Even Christians racked by this reality wonder if they can still trust God when there is so much evil in the world. Clearly, those who affirm that God is in control of all things and is working everything in accordance with his good and wise eternal plan must face the very serious problem of the existence of terrible evil and tragic suffering in the world.

Some offer solutions to the problem of evil that simply don't work. One inadequate solution is to deny that evil exists. For example, Hindus believe that evil is *maya,* or illusion; there is no such thing as pain and suffering. Similarly, Christian Scientists (a cult that is neither Christian nor scientific) claim that evil does not exist; it is only bad thinking. The founder of Christian Scientism, Mary Baker

Eddy, says: "Evil is but an illusion, and it has no real basis. Evil is false belief."[1] Please explain that to one of my childhood friends whose father—a Christian Scientist—came down with a very curable disease but refused medical help. He believed his sickness was only a wrong idea. Now bad ideas usually don't cost people their lives—but my friend's father needlessly died from his illness. Illusionism is overturned by the hard reality of evil.

Another unsatisfying solution is acquiescence, or passive acceptance, of the problem of evil. Atheists find themselves with this solution. Because there is no God, and because evil is just part of the world, there can be no problem of evil. People must simply accept its reality and resign themselves to the tragedy and heartache evil brings. No hope exists for a resolution. Buddhism believes that pain and suffering are an irremovable part of the continuous cycle of birth, death, and rebirth. As long as people exist in this cycle, they must simply accept the reality of evil. The only hope of escape is by ridding themselves of all attachment to worldly things. Only by this extremely difficult path of self-denial can people achieve peace and happiness, or nirvana. Otherwise, they are consigned to a life of suffering and pain. Resignation in the face of evil, however, imagines that evil is an inherent part of human existence—it's just the way life is—and it fails to point to God as the ultimate hope for victory over evil.

Explaining Evil

The church has always wrestled with the problem of evil, attempting to develop an explanation for the existence of evil in relationship to God. Any such attempt is called a *theodicy*. A theodicy (*theos* means "God" and *dike* means "justification") is a defense of God in light of the presence of evil. It attempts to justify why God allows evil or does not remove evil from the world.

The Philosophical Problem of Evil

One theodicy deals with *the philosophical problem of evil* as framed by the famous skeptic David Hume in the eighteenth century:

Is God willing to prevent evil, but not able? Then he is impotent.

Is he able, but not willing? Then he is malevolent.
Is he both able and willing? Whence then is evil?[2]

Let's analyze Hume's presentation. The problem of evil questions either the omnipotence of God, the goodness of God, or the existence of evil. (1) If we grant that evil exists, and if we believe that God is good so as to want to stop evil, then we must conclude that God is not powerful enough to do what he wants to do. He is impotent to eliminate evil from the world. (2) If we grant that evil exists, and if we believe that God is powerful enough to stop evil, then we must conclude that God is not really good at all. He must be malevolent or evil instead because he doesn't want to stop it. (3) If we believe that God is both powerful enough to stop evil and good so as to want to stop evil, then we must conclude either that evil doesn't exist or be completely without explanation for its reality.

To put it a bit differently, the problem of evil means that we can believe in two of the following three statements, but not all three:

1. God is all-powerful.
2. God is completely good.
3. Evil exists.

Because point three is certain—we don't accept illusionism and deny the existence of evil—we must either give up God as being all-powerful (point one) or God as being completely good (point two). In either case, we are not left with the vision of God that the church has always held.

In response to the philosophical problem of evil, the church offers a four-step theodicy.[3] The *first step* is to carefully define the omnipotence of God, or what we mean when we say that God is all-powerful. As we have discussed, God's omnipotence means that he can do all that he as God is able to do. We do not mean that God can do absolutely everything, because God is not able to do certain things—for example, he cannot sleep or cease to exist. An important point for our discussion is that God cannot create a world that contains two contradictory realities. For example, God cannot create a world in which I am married to Nora and where Nora does not exist. These two realities are contradictory, or mutually exclusive—they cannot exist together. This would be absurd, and even our omnipotent God cannot do absurdities.

The *second step* is to note that in creating a world, God had to choose between actualizing one of two good things. Because they are two contradictory realities, God could not actualize both of them together. The two good things God chose between were:

- Option 1: a world in which there is no evil. (Obviously, this world would be a good world. So option 1 was a good option that God could have chosen when creating a world.)
- Option 2: a world in which some other good thing exists along with evil.

A number of ideas are offered for this second option. Some believe that the other good option that God could have chosen is a world in which human beings have free will. Of course, if God grants free will, then he runs the risk that we will use our free will to do evil. That is, we could choose freely to love God and worship him, or we could choose freely to hate God and turn against him. But at least human beings have free will, which is a good thing. Some propose that the other good option that God could have chosen is a world in which human beings grow from self-centered people to spiritually and morally mature people characterized by courage, mercy, and forgiveness. Of course, if those qualities are to develop, evil is necessary. Adversity and trials foster mature character, which is a good thing. In every case, whatever people envision as the other good thing that God wanted to bring about in creating a world, that good thing is dependent on the presence of evil in the world.

My personal preference for this second option is to see the other good thing as the preservation of people as the sort of human beings God created. He created us as human beings with the capacity to think, an ability to feel emotions, a will to decide and to act, creativity to form intentions, and a structure for bodily movement. For God to intervene suddenly and eliminate evil from the world, he would have to disrupt human existence as he created it to be. Imagine that Joe thinks about harming another person. To eliminate that evil, God would have to numb that portion of Joe's mind so he no longer thinks about hurting someone. Or suppose that Jane has hatched a detailed plot to rob a store. To eliminate that evil, God would have to press the delete button in Jane's intentionality. Or picture John actually beginning to pull the trigger to kill someone. To eliminate that evil, God would have to break John's thumb so he couldn't squeeze the gun. In each and every case, human existence as we know and experience it would be radically altered. We would no longer be the sort of human beings God created.

God had a choice between creating a world in which there is no evil or a world in which some other good thing exists along with evil. He could not do both because the two are contradictory realities. On the one hand, if God decides to create a world in which there is no evil, he does a good thing. But human beings would not have free will. Or we could not develop from self-centered people to spiritually and morally mature people. Indeed, if God would eliminate evil, we would no longer be the sort of human beings God created. On the other hand, if God decides to create a world in which these things take place, he does a good thing. But the world could not be without evil, for evil is necessary in these cases.

The *third step* is an appeal to a common ethical principle: No one can be held morally responsible for failing to do what he could not do. For example, you are swimming in a lake and suddenly see two people drowning. You are an excellent swimmer and know you can save one victim, but you cannot save both. You dive in, swim to one, and save that victim, but the other person drowns. You save one, and for this you are praised. No one would find you guilty of failing to save the second person, because you could not save both.

If we apply this common ethical principle to our second step, God is not able to both create a world in which there is no evil and create a world in which some other good thing exists along with evil. He can choose one or the other, but not both. No matter which option he chooses, he cannot be found guilty for failing to create both worlds. This means that if God decides to create a world in which human beings have free will or grow from self-centered people to spiritually and morally mature people or continue to be the sort of human beings God intended to and did indeed create, he cannot be held responsible for not creating a world in which there is no evil.

The *fourth step* is to affirm that the option God did indeed choose—option 2, a world in which some other good thing exists along with evil—is as good as, or even better than, option 1, a world in which there is no evil. Imagine that we place these two options on a scale of justice. The value of the world in which we live—the world with its pain and suffering, adversities and trials—either counterbalances or overbalances the other possible world without evil. In creating our world, therefore, God has done no wrong. Therefore we can affirm these three truths and hold them together:

1. God is all-powerful.
2. God is completely good.
3. Evil exists.

This is the theodicy for the philosophical problem of evil.

PAUSE TIME— Do you have friends who are wrestling with the philosophical problem of evil? Perhaps it is the reason they doubt or deny God's existence. Could this theodicy be helpful to them?

The Theological Problem of Evil

While many people, both believers and unbelievers alike, wrestle with the philosophical problem of evil as discussed above, most Christians want to understand the biblical teaching on God's relationship to the evil in this world. We could call this the *theological problem of evil* because it deals with pain and suffering from the perspective of Scripture.

Beginning with Genesis 1, we note that evil was not part of God's original creation. Having completed his creative activity, "God saw all that he had made, and it was very good" (Genesis 1:31). We would be hard-pressed to take this divine assessment and conclude that evil was present from the very beginning of creation.

Rather, evil was introduced sometime after the original creation came to be. But why, and how?

Genesis 3 answers the *how* question as it recounts the origin of sin in the human race. Though focused on eating the fruit from the tree of the knowledge of good and evil, the fall of our original parents involved pride, disobedience, and unfaithfulness. But why would Adam and Eve—who enjoyed a face-to-face relationship with God, complete intimacy with one another, and a harmonious existence with all of creation—decide to throw all this away? The story indicates that Eve was tricked into sinning; yet, how could this occur in an ideal world? Even before evil was introduced among human beings, it was already present in the cunning deceit of the serpent. Of course, at work behind this crafty creature was "the ancient serpent, who is called the Devil and Satan, the one who deceives the whole world" (Revelation 12:9). He provoked Adam and Eve to sin by questioning the word of God, casting doubt upon God's goodness, and blatantly denying the deadly consequences of rebellion. We can therefore say that sin entered into human experience through the trickery of our enemy Satan. But that only pushes back the question of why there is evil in our experience to why previously there was evil in the angelic realm.

Though Scripture does not indicate much to help us with the *why* question, it does portray God's relationship to the evil that is present in the world. As we have already seen, God's sovereign plan encompasses the evil plans and actions of people: "The Lord works out everything for his own ends—even the wicked for a day of disaster" (Proverbs 16:4).

The story of Joseph and the drama of Jesus' crucifixion illustrate God's use of evil deeds and wicked people to accomplish his wise and good purpose for the world. In both cases (and in many others as well) the people who carry out the evil—Joseph's brothers who sell him into slavery, and the major players who condemned Jesus to death and crucified him—are held morally accountable for the wrong they do. God does not do evil, nor does he force people to do the evil they do, but he uses the evil people commit to bring about his plan.

But there is more. At times, God proactively raises up evil, especially to punish sin. An example of this is when God brings disaster upon his people Israel because of their idolatry: "This is what the LORD says: 'I am going to bring disaster on this place and its people. . . . Because they have forsaken me and burned incense to other gods and provoked me to anger by all the idols their hands have made, my anger will burn against this place and will not be quenched'" (2 Kings 22:16–17).

God planned to bring about this disaster by raising up the treacherous army of the Babylonians (Habakkuk 1:5–6). The surprising nature of this divine act was not lost on Habakkuk. He questioned why God, who is absolutely holy, would use such an evil instrument to punish his own relatively good people:

O LORD, you have appointed them to execute judgment;
O Rock, you have ordained them to punish.
Your eyes are too pure to look on evil;
you cannot tolerate wrong.
Why then do you tolerate the treacherous?
Why are you silent while the wicked
swallow up those more righteous than themselves?
(Habakkuk 1:12–13)

Certainly, Habakkuk expresses *our* objection to God's involvement with wicked people and evil acts. It seems wrong to us that God, who is perfectly holy, could be closely associated with evil; holiness and wickedness seem to be mutually exclusive. We feel very uncomfortable with such a close link between God and evil.

Our sense that something is wrong with this picture points us to an important truth about the relationship between God and evil. Even when the Bible describes God's involvement with evil, it never ascribes blame to God for evil. And God is never presented as taking pleasure in evil. Rather, the blame is always placed on human beings (or, at times, on angelic beings like Satan) for the evil they carry out or the evil they provoke. For example, in the story of Joseph, his brothers are to blame for the evil they brought about against Joseph. In the Babylonian captivity, the idolatry of the people of Israel is to blame for the terrible destruction of their nation by the treacherous Babylonians. In the drama of Jesus' crucifixion, Herod, Pontius Pilate, the Roman soldiers, and the religious leaders of the Jews are held morally accountable for the conspiracy and act of treachery against Jesus.

We should never imagine that God delights in bringing about evil, and we should never blame God for using evil. Rather, we should blame ourselves or others who carry out evil. Though God employs evil for his purposes, he is never to be blamed for evil. Why this is so is a great mystery! One way of understanding it is to make a distinction between *primary causes* and *secondary causes*. God is the *primary cause* of all things as he sovereignly works out his good and wise plan in and through everything. Human beings (and, at times, angelic beings) are *secondary causes* who freely and responsibly decide and act and are therefore held morally accountable for the evil they commit. The primary cause is more remote from evil (shown in the diagram by being further away from evil), while the secondary causes are closer to evil (again, shown in the diagram):

primary cause (God)   secondary causes (human beings)   evil

As the primary cause of all things—even evil—God is further removed from it and so is not to blame for the evil that occurs. The secondary causes—human beings (and, at times, angels and demons)—who are closer in proximity to it receive all the blame for the evil that occurs.

This may be at the heart of why we say that God *causes* all the good things that happen in this world but he *permits* all the evil things that take place. Again, this sense that we need to distinguish between divine *causation* and divine *permission* expresses an important truth. God receives all the credit for whatever good occurs in the world. We recognize that he is at work to bring about the good, and we rightly praise him for it. That is his relationship to good. But his relationship to evil is such that he does not receive blame for whatever evil occurs in the world. We recognize that though he is ultimately at work even when evil is present, we cannot blame him for it.

Yet, it is very important not to press this distinction too far. When we say that God *causes* good but *permits* evil, we should never view evil as having a life of its own. We should never think that God does not have complete control over all the evil that occurs. We should never imagine that God is working out his Plan A but becomes stuck when evil arises, so he has to abandon Plan A and shift to Plan B to allow evil to take place. If we say that God sovereignly and in accordance with his wise plan permits evil to occur, we are on solid ground. But if we say that at best God allows evil to occur because it is somehow outside of his sovereignty, or that God doesn't choose for evil to occur because it is foreign to his wise plan, then we are on shaky ground.

Even this explanation fails to explain adequately the mystery of why God's close association with evil results in no blame for him but always for us. But some things we know for sure—evil was not part of his original creation, and God is sovereign over both good and evil: "Is it not from the mouth of the Most High that both calamities (evil things) and good things come?" (Lamentations 3:38).

At times, God himself raises up evil, especially to punish sin. Still, God is never to be blamed for the evil that he uses; rather, we who do evil receive the blame. If we want to press the point further and complain that it seems unfair—after all, the evil for which we are blamed is ultimately part of the eternal plan of our sovereign God—we are told to not go there: "You will say to me, therefore, 'Why then does He still find fault? For who can resist His will?' But who are you—anyone who talks back to God? Will what is formed say to the one who formed it, 'Why did you make me like this?'" (Romans 9:19–20). As created beings designed by God in a fitting way, we must put our fingers over our mouths and remain silent. We accept our human status before our Creator God. Period. Mystery surrounds this reality of God and evil, and we must not stray beyond what we know for sure.

But this is not the end of the story.

God's sovereign plan for this evil-stained world ends with the ultimate triumph of his greatness and goodness over all evil of every kind. In an awesome vision, John describes the return of Jesus Christ to utterly defeat all the wicked enemies of God:

I saw heaven opened, and there was a white horse! Its
rider is called Faithful and True, and in righteousness He
judges and makes war. His eyes were like a fiery flame,
and on His head were many crowns. He had a name written that no one knows except Himself. He wore a robe
stained with blood, and His name is called the Word of
God. The armies that were in heaven followed Him on
white horses, wearing pure white linen. From His mouth
came a sharp sword, so that with it He might strike the
nations. He will shepherd them with an iron scepter. He
will also trample the winepress of the fierce anger of God,
the Almighty. And on His robe and on His thigh He has a
name written:

> KING OF KINGS
> AND LORD OF LORDS

(Revelation 19:11–16)

Even death, the hideous last enemy, will itself be destroyed, and
the triumphant Jesus Christ will turn everything over to the Father:
"Then comes the end, when [Christ] hands over the kingdom to
God the Father, when He abolishes all rule and all authority and
power. . . . The last enemy He abolishes is death. . . . And when
everything is subject to Him, then the Son Himself will also be subject to Him who subjected everything to Him, so that God may be
all in all" (1 Corinthians 15:24, 26, 28).

It is with this hope of the ultimate defeat of evil by our Lord and
King that we face and overcome suffering and pain in the world in
which we live.

 How do you feel about God's close
association with evil? Does it give you
hope that no trouble can come your
way, no evil can befall you, except as our good and wise God
wills it to happen? Do you think this truth will help you to
trust and thank God when you face pain and suffering?

For Those Who Suffer

CHAPTER 12

Abel is killed by his brother Cain.

Noah is mocked and spurned by ungodly people as he preaches about righteousness during his building of the ark.

Isaac is such a successful farmer and herdsman that the Philistines sabotage his water source and force him to move elsewhere.

Pretending to be his brother, Jacob deceives his father Isaac and receives the family inheritance that rightly belongs to Esau.

Laban promises that he will give his daughter Rachel to Jacob in marriage if Jacob will work for him for seven years; but after the time passes, Laban substitutes his daughter Leah. It costs Jacob another seven years of work to get Rachel as his wife as well.

Joseph is sold into slavery by his jealous brothers.

Shadrach, Meshach, and Abednego are thrown into a blazing furnace as punishment for their refusal to worship the image of Nebuchadnezzar.

All the boys in Bethlehem and its vicinity under the age of two years are slaughtered with the expectation that Jesus would be killed as well.

The innocent Son of God is crucified at the hands of evil men.

Stephen is stoned to death by a mob of angry Jews, becoming the first Christian martyr.

The apostles Paul and Peter are executed during the reign of Emperor Nero.

At the age of eighty-eight, Polycarp is burned at the stake for refusing to deny Christ and worship the Roman gods.

Perpetua, a young pregnant woman, is thrust through with a sword and martyred for her Christian faith.

Regular, systematic persecutions of Christians take place during the first three hundred years of the church's existence.

Six million Jews are slaughtered by the Nazis during World War II.

Cassie Bernall, a dedicated believer, and five other teenagers are gunned down by two fellow students at Columbine High School.

On September 11, 2001, thousands of people—Christians, Jews, Muslims, Hindus, agnostics, atheists—lose their lives as terrorists hijack planes and crash them into the World Trade Center towers and the Pentagon.

The Heartache of Suffering

Obviously, this list could be multiplied by billions of entries. Even then, we would only succeed in expressing in writing what we all know to be a well-established and tragically experienced fact—life is full of suffering. From the death of loved ones to the loss of a job, from the failure of a marriage to persecution for being a Christian, from the disastrous consequences of sin to a persistent illness, we all experience the heartache of suffering.

The Personal Problem of Evil

In the previous chapter, I looked at both the philosophical problem of evil and the theological problem of evil. Now I want to consider the *personal problem of evil*. Why do we personally suffer? Why do our friends, family members, neighbors, fellow students, and colleagues at work experience personal pain and tragedy? Beyond the *why* question, *how* should we as Christians respond when we personally suffer? And how can we best help others when they encounter pain and tragedy?

Reasons for Suffering

The Bible presents many reasons for suffering. I will focus on four key ones: Suffering occurs as a result of sin, as an opportunity to glorify God, as a spiritual wake-up call, and as an opportunity to build godly character. We may often have a difficult time understanding why specific cases of suffering occur, and we should be careful in jumping to conclusions in this area. But the Bible helps us to see the reasons why suffering strikes us and others.

Result of Sin

As we have seen in the last chapter, some suffering comes as a result of sin; it is God's way of judging disobedience and punishing faithlessness. This is true only of *some* suffering. I want to emphasize this because one of our tendencies is to jump immediately to the conclusion that when others or we suffer, the suffering is due to sin on their part or ours. Even Jesus encountered this pervasive attitude from his own disciples during his ministry, but he offered a different explanation for suffering: "As [Jesus] was passing by, He saw a man blind from birth. His disciples questioned Him: 'Rabbi, who sinned, this man or his parents, that he was born blind?' 'Neither this man sinned nor his parents,' Jesus answered. 'This came about so that God's works might be displayed in him'" (John 9:1–3). In this case, the blindness this man suffered was not due to any sin, but it became the occasion for Jesus to work a miracle by restoring this man's sight.

We should be cautious, then, in automatically thinking that suffering is caused by sin. Jumping to the conclusion that a person suffering from AIDS is being punished by God for homosexual activity would be incorrect if that victim received tainted blood during a routine and necessary surgical operation. At the same time, we should not fall into the other extreme of dismissing any and all suffering as being the result of sin. If a drunk person gets behind the wheel of an automobile and recklessly crashes into another car, wounding or killing its passengers, that suffering is directly the result of the sin of drunkenness.

Opportunity to Glorify God

In the above story, Jesus uncovers another reason for suffering: It provides an opportunity for God to demonstrate his mighty power. This reason may sound harsh and self-serving because it seems that personal suffering is just a setup for God to act so as to gain attention. We could even complain, "But God, certainly other ways exist for you to prove your power and receive the honor you are due than by having people suffer!" I think it is safe to say that many ways exist for God to express his might so as to receive his rightful glory. But we also affirm that God is a perfectly wise God—he always chooses

 **PAUSE TIME—** Let me challenge you with this question, one that goes to the very heart of what it means to live under the lordship of Jesus Christ: If you knew that your suffering is God's very best for you and will ultimately result in him receiving the greatest glory—and you could not have his best in any other way—would you be willing to suffer for the sake of his honor?

That's a hard one—for you, for me, for everyone! It may be one of the most difficult questions you will ever have to answer, and it is one that all of us who call Jesus our Lord must wrestle with throughout our lives. And you are not alone in sensing how hard it is to answer yes to it. Even as I type these words, I have many reservations race through my head as I want to reaffirm my basic commitment to the question, "Am I willing to suffer for the sake of God's honor?" What will it mean if I say yes? What will it mean if you say yes? What will it cost me? What will it cost you? Immediately we think of great sacrifices God will ask us to make—giving up certain friends, suffering physical and/or emotional pain, changing the dreams we have for our lives, adopting a new purpose, being persecuted for our Christian commitment, experiencing the tragic loss of loved ones, reorienting the direction of our lives so it is all about God and not about ourselves. Are we truly willing to undergo these and other possible experiences for the sake of bringing great glory to God?

When my wife and I first said yes to this question, it came in this form: "Are you willing to go anywhere, say anything, do anything, and give up everything—cost whatever it may cost—for the sake of Jesus Christ?" By faith we said yes. Within two years God asked us to leave our families, friends, a thriving ministry, the promise of money to pay for further education and to buy a house, and our country to become missionaries in Europe. We had to learn a new language, adapt to a new culture, make new friends, be misunderstood and misdirected, rarely see our families, live with isolation and loneliness, and experience both great times in ministry and very dark periods. Did we suffer? It was the hardest period of our lives—and we haven't come close to duplicating the difficulties since then. Was God glorified? At certain times, in very concrete ways, he was. But we have many, many questions about the other times—honestly, it is hard to see how. If we could go back in time and do it all over again, would we change our decision and choose a different path? Absolutely not. When we said yes to God, we yielded the rights to our lives and we agreed to anything and everything—including suffering—that he would bring our way. That was absolutely the right thing to do. Whatever it cost us in terms of suffering, we know that we could not have had God's best any other way.

If you knew that your suffering is God's very best for you and will ultimately result in him receiving the greatest glory—and you could not have his best in any other way—would you be willing to suffer for the sake of his honor? Think very carefully before you answer this question. Please do not say no—why live as a compromised Christian and waste your life? Please do not say yes because I want you to, or because others say yes, or because you think it would please your parents, or because you imagine that you can always change your mind later—God doesn't like broken promises. Instead, ask God to make you a courageous Christian who is willing to lay it all on the line for his glory. Then you will say yes and mean it. And here's God's promise to you: "Those who honor me I will honor" (1 Samuel 2:30).

the best goals and the best ways to accomplish those goals for his greatest glory. This has to mean that in each case of personal tragedy, the path of suffering is the best means to accomplish God's wise goal so as to bring him the greatest glory. We could not experience God's best if the path was not one of suffering.

Spiritual Wake-Up Call

Another reason for suffering is that it urges us to turn toward God. As C. S. Lewis notes, pain is God's megaphone to get our attention and urge us to find him.[1]

This is true for people who are not yet Christians. For instance, take self-sufficient people who have constructed satisfying lives for themselves. They are able to provide all the necessities of life—as well as many luxuries—by their own efforts. They surround themselves with security measures to shelter themselves from pain and suffering. God is the last thing they think about. To destroy the artificial props that support their self-sufficiency, God brings tragedy into their lives. In some cases, the wake-up call goes unheeded. In other cases, God gets their attention through suffering.

This is also true for us Christians. When we go astray, God disciplines us, often through the experience of pain and suffering. The writer to the Hebrews gives us a lengthy explanation of this:

"'My son, do not take the Lord's discipline lightly,
or faint when you are reproved by Him;
for the Lord disciplines whom He loves,
and punishes every son whom He receives.'
Endure it as discipline: God is dealing with you as sons. For what son is there whom a father does not discipline? But if you are without discipline—which all receive—then you are illegitimate children and not sons. . . . He does it for our benefit, so that we can share His holiness. No discipline seems enjoyable at the time, but painful. Later on, however, it yields the fruit of peace and righteousness to those who have been trained by it" (Hebrews 12:5–8, 10–11).

Being disciplined by God is hard, unpleasant, and very painful at times. Yet the purpose for discipline is a wise and encouraging one—God designs it for our good. Suffering drives home the lesson that the sin in our lives is desperately wrong, and it urges us to break with sin and do what is right. The results of discipline are what we desire—we become imitators of God's holiness as we become more and more like him! No wonder the writer of Hebrews encourages us to willingly accept suffering that comes as God's discipline.

Opportunity to Build Godly Character

We may suffer hardships and trials even when we are not being disciplined for wrong attitudes and actions. These experiences of suffering are intended to develop a mature character in us that lasts throughout our entire lifetime, in both good times and difficult times. The apostle Paul explains this: "We rejoice in the hope of the glory of God. And not only that, but we also rejoice in our afflictions, because we know that affliction produces endurance, endurance produces proven character, and proven character produces hope. This hope does not disappoint, because God's love has been poured out in our hearts through the Holy Spirit who was given to us" (Romans 5:2–5).

James has something similar to say: "Consider it a great joy, my brothers, whenever you experience various trials, knowing that the testing of your faith produces endurance. But endurance must do its complete work, so that you may be mature and complete, lacking nothing" (James 1:2–4).

Facing trials and suffering through tough times results in a progressive development. It begins with perseverance—we learn to stick with God and endure the ups and downs of life. As we walk faithfully with God through difficult times, a solid character of integrity and genuineness develops. With this, maturity and completeness progress as we become all that God means for us to be. Hope is developed—we become convinced that this growth will continue throughout our lives.

 So what is God's strategy for developing you into a strong follower of Jesus Christ? Though it involves many things, one element in his plan is adversity and trials. You just can't have what God needs to develop in you apart from suf-

fering. Sometimes it will come because you are disobedient and God needs to straighten you out. Other times suffering will come your way not because you have gone wrong but because trials create the environment for you to become courageous, resilient under pressure, and full of hope.

Think back to when you were going the wrong way. How did God discipline you to get you back on the right track? What was your response to his discipline? What was the outcome of his discipline? Think about trials you have faced that were not due to sin on your part. Perhaps you've clashed with a family member who just can't seem to understand and respect you. Perhaps you've lost a close friend because of your commitment to Christ. Perhaps you've put forth a great deal of effort in a certain class or in training for a sport, but the desired results just won't come. What is God trying to work into your life? What lesson does he want you to learn? How are you a different—and hopefully better—person today because of your difficulties? Is this reason to thank God?

So How Should Christians Respond to Personal Suffering?

When we suffer, we should acknowledge that God is in complete control of our desperate situation and never blame God for the evil that comes our way. Despite persistent thoughts to the contrary, we should praise him for working his good and wise plan. We should fight the tendency to question God's sovereignty. One way of doing this is to trust the promise Paul offers us: "We know that all things work together for the good of those who love God: those who are called according to his purpose" (Romans 8:28). When we cling to this promise, we are not trying to convince ourselves that pain and suffering are good things—quite the contrary! Rather, while acknowledging that the events that happen to us are indeed difficult, we further recognize that God uses those difficulties to accomplish his good in our lives. Another important way of acknowledging God's control is to refuse to blame him.

Beyond this, we should be thankful to God when we suffer. Thanksgiving should be a lifestyle for us Christians. Paul urges us to "give thanks in everything, for this is God's will for you in Christ Jesus" (1 Thessalonians 5:18). Indeed, as we are guided by the Holy Spirit, we are "giving thanks always for everything to God the Father in the name of our Lord Jesus Christ" (Ephesians 5:20). If thankfulness is to characterize our lives, then it should be true of us even when we suffer. James encourages this: "Consider it a great joy, my brothers, whenever you experience various trials, knowing that the testing of your faith produces endurance" (James 1:2–3). Paul adds: "We rejoice in the hope of the glory of God. And not only that, but we also rejoice in our afflictions, because we know that affliction produces endurance, endurance produces proven character, and proven character produces hope. This hope does not disappoint, because God's love has been poured out in our hearts through the Holy Spirit who was given to us" (Romans 5:2–5). We are able to give thanks because we see the good purpose at work in our suffering. And when we suffer, the hope that we develop connects us with the powerful experience of the love of God.

As we thank God in the midst of hardship, we should never pretend that we don't really suffer or that we enjoy suffering. I emphasize this because some Christians think it is wrong to ever think that some event or circumstance is indeed painful. They develop a kind of denial—suffering, if it does exist, doesn't impact them. This stoic response toward hardship is both dishonest and unproductive, not to mention unrealistic.

We should also not be afraid to be completely honest with God about our feelings when we suffer. David becomes a model for us in his prayer to God in the midst of great pain:

How long, O LORD? Will you forget me forever?
How long will you hide your face from me?
How long must I wrestle with my thoughts
and every day have sorrow in my heart?
How long will my enemy triumph over me?
Look on me and answer, O LORD my God.
Give light to my eyes, or I will sleep in death;

my enemy will say, "I have overcome him,"
　　and my foes will rejoice when I fall.
But I will trust in your unfailing love;
　　my heart rejoices in your salvation.
I will sing to the LORD, for he has been good to me. (Psalm 13)

With brutal honesty, David complains to God. He is sick and tired of his difficulties. He feels completely abandoned by God—he has no sense of God's comfort and concern. In addition, David protests against his enemies getting the upper hand. They are laughing over his demise, making David look bad—not to mention God, who is supposed to be caring for him. David feels that his life is over—indeed, unless God does something, he will die. But notice how David concludes. Having poured out his heart and complaints and tears, David joyfully expresses his unfailing faith in God's unfailing love.

Trust and truthfulness are not mutually exclusive attitudes for us to have. We can be completely transparent with God in voicing our objections and complaints, without fear of reprisal. God is not shocked by the feelings of abandonment and disappointment that we express to him—indeed, because he knows us completely, he realizes how upset we are even if we don't say anything. What doesn't help is to be dishonest with God, telling him what we think he wants to hear—"Thank you for my sufferings; I really enjoy pain and grief!"—when that is not at all how we feel. Let's follow the model of David—as we truthfully and tearfully cry out to God, let's also affirm our trust in his love.

How Should Christians Respond to Others' Suffering?

If this is how we Christians should respond when we personally suffer, how can we best help others when they encounter pain and tragedy? We should first realize that each person is different. This means each one will respond to suffering differently and need a different kind of help from us. I can't tell you what to do in each individual case, but I can offer a few things to consider when someone we know experiences suffering. Some of these are *things not to do,* and some are *things to do.*

Things Not to Do

First, we shouldn't tell others that we know exactly how they feel. Even if our sufferings arise from similar circumstances—perhaps it is the loss of a family member, or the divorce of parents—different people react in different ways. Because feelings are personal matters, it is hard to imagine that any two people ever feel exactly the same thing even in similar circumstances. Also, those who say this tend to launch into a lengthy description of their tragedy, drawing attention to themselves and not helping the one who is suffering. I'm not minimizing the importance of empathizing with others or sharing their feelings, but there are better ways of doing so.

Second, we shouldn't imagine that we know why others are suffering. This is both presumptuous and dangerous! Because some people want to resolve others' problems, they seek to identify the cause of the problems so they can offer a concrete solution. It's almost like a medical diagnosis—the patients are suffering X, so they must have done Y. But because suffering arises for many different reasons, it is difficult to say with precision that any particular case of suffering is due to this or that particular reason. Thus, it is presumptuous to think we know the answer to the why question. Also, what if we are wrong in identifying the reason for others' suffering? One of the most common errors in working with people who suffer is to ascribe their suffering to some personal sin on their part. As we have seen, only some suffering is due to this reason. If we link their suffering with some personal sin on their part, then they are completely to blame for the tragic situation in which they find themselves. Imagine the feelings of guilt that arise from this! They then renounce their supposed sin and try not to do it again, but they continue to suffer. Therefore they try harder, with the same result. Guilty feelings are multiplied, and often desperation or resignation sets in—and it is all due to a wrong diagnosis in the first place. This can be very dangerous.

Third, we shouldn't minimize the pain and suffering of others by insisting that their situation really isn't as bad as they think it is. Some suffering is due to very knotty problems that take years of great effort to untie. Plus, this can give a false idea that if they just think positively about their suffering, it will go away. How untrue and cruel! Also, this may encourage them to play the stoic and not to be honest with God and others about their pain. David's model stands against this. We also shouldn't tell people that if they just have enough faith, God will bless them and they will stop suffering. While it is very important to live with a strong faith when suffering, it may be the case that God's mysterious plan is for them to suffer. Faith and suffering are not mutually exclusive.

Finally, we should never allow the sufferings of others to lead to doing evil. Though at the onset of tragedy the tendency may be to curse God, we have seen how very wrong it is to ever blame God. Also, some people who are desperately suffering express a desire to be dead or even kill themselves. Often this is due to deep depression, which can be treated medically and with counseling. We should not allow others to do anything—such as refuse to take prescribed medicine, or arrange for a physician to assist with suicide— that would cause a premature death to escape the pain they are in.

Things to Do

There are some positive things we can do. First, we should realize that sometimes the best help we can give may appear to be no help at all. Several years ago one of my dear friends thanked me for coming to his mother's funeral many years earlier. He recalled it with great fondness and comfort; just my presence in that time of tragedy meant so much to him. All I could recall was how terrified I was at the thought of going to the funeral. I feel very uncomfortable in these situations and am often at loss for words. I remembered how I tried to think of excuses not to go. When those excuses failed, I tried to think of how to avoid my friend so I wouldn't fumble my words and make a fool of myself. But I did go and did embrace my friend, expressing only how sorry I was for the loss of his mother. But that was all that was needed. What appeared to be of no help at all turned out to be of benefit. So, as we are with people who are suffering, we shouldn't immediately think of what we have to do to be of help. Perhaps just our being with them is all that is needed at the time.

Second, we should help people to know that God himself is not unfamiliar with suffering. After all, he gave up his own Son to be crucified as the innocent God-man at the hands of the same wicked human beings whom he came to save. The death of Christ is convincing proof that God himself is intimately acquainted with pain and tragedy. And because Jesus Christ has suffered, he is completely prepared to sympathize with us when we suffer: "We do not have a high priest who is unable to sympathize with our weaknesses, but One who has been tested in every way as we are, yet without sin. Therefore let us approach the throne of grace with boldness, so that we may receive mercy and find grace to help us at the proper time" (Hebrews 4:15–16). We are invited to find help in times of suffering from the one who himself has suffered like we do. God is no stranger to tragedy, and Jesus Christ is ready to give mercy and grace to help us in troubled times.

Third, we should also remind other Christians that God is good enough and powerful enough to bring good out of the very worst evil. This is his promise: "We know that all things work together for the good of those who love God: those who are called according to his purpose" (Romans 8:28). We can encourage others that their suffering is God's master plan, tailor-made for their ultimate good. Though they don't and often can't see the good that he has designed through the instrument of pain and tragedy, we can offer sure words of hope that God is working for their good. We should pray that, by faith, they will accept their suffering as being under the control of our great and loving God.

PAUSE TIME— A word of caution: We have looked at some awesome truths about God, suffering, and comfort. As Christians, these are so important to us that we naturally and rightly want to communicate them to others. As we do this, however, we should pay attention to how we do it. At times, sharing the Word of God can come across to those who suffer as merely offering pat answers, a panacea for all our troubles. Perhaps this is due in part to our tendency to simply read a passage and then expect an immediate response that deals with the suffering once and for all. This may happen, but in many cases it doesn't take place. In fact, this approach can backfire and be counterproductive. It can come across as being impersonal, even coldhearted. Those who suffer need and deserve more than mere Christian clichés. They need and deserve compassion, heartfelt sympathy, sharing of the sorrow and burden, and a patient and consistent companionship to walk the path of suffering with them. This takes more than just offering words, no matter how true the Word is.

Discovering God's Will for Your Life

CHAPTER 13

Between graduation from college and our wedding, my wife and I spent several weeks raising support for our upcoming work with Campus Crusade for Christ. One day we visited a businessman in a small town outside of South Bend, Indiana. As we explained our future plans for ministry with students, our friend commented on how interesting it would be if we ended up at ND—the University of Notre Dame, right there in South Bend. It was a joke—Notre Dame is a Catholic university, and Campus Crusade is a Protestant movement—and we all laughed heartily together!

Having finished our conversation, we walked to our car for the drive back to Chicago. My wife opened the passenger-side door and climbed in, and I opened the driver-side door and sat down. We turned, looked at each other, and said simultaneously and without consulting each other, "God wants us to be at Notre Dame." Mysteriously, but clearly and decisively, God took the businessman's joking comment and used it to direct us to our first ministry with Campus Crusade. To this day we don't understand it, but God gave us a very strong conviction that we were to go to Notre Dame—and that is where we ended up for two years.

As we were cruising along in our work at ND, we sensed the tug of God to spend a summer overseas working with Campus Crusade in Italy. We signed up for a six-week summer project in

Rome and began to make preparations for our trip. One afternoon, as I was returning from the South Bend library with books on the Italian language and culture, my wife greeted me at the front door of our home and handed me the phone. "*You* better talk with them!" she said cryptically. On the other end of the line was one of the international directors of Campus Crusade. "That's great that you're getting books about Italy," he said encouragingly, "because you're going to need them. Not only for your six-week summer project, however. We want you to go to Italy on a five-year assignment." We would eventually spend seven years in both Italy and the Italian-speaking part of Switzerland.

Knowing God's Will

I don't think I've ever met a Christian who doesn't wonder—and even worry—about how we know God's will for our lives. I can't offer any easy, pat answers to this important issue. Looking at my own experience recounted in the stories above, God directed me through a mysterious, inward conviction when telling me to go to ND and through an ordinary long-distance phone call from my supervisors when telling me to go to Italy. In addition to these ways, God has also directed me through the wise (and not-so-wise) counsel of friends, by helping me to understand where best to use my spiritual gifts, by opening certain doors and closing others, through encouraging me to honor previously-made commitments, and by many other ways. Obviously, then, I don't know a secret formula for knowing God's will. But I can offer you some insights to help.

Because you are who you are, you face the most important decisions of your life right now and in the future. What kind of a person—independent from your parents, that is—are you going to be? Why kind of mark will you leave on your friends, classmates, family, teachers, colleagues at work, fellow athletes, neighbors, and people at church during your high school years? Does your future career include attending college—and, if so, which one—or moving directly into the workforce? After you've changed jobs several times, what will you finally settle on doing? Will you get married or remain single? If the former, why should you marry, who will you marry, when will you get married, and how can you get married? In the latter case, how will you control your physical desires, and how can you overcome loneliness? Will you have a family, how many kids will you have, how will you support them, where will you raise them, and how can you be a good parent to them? How can you thrive as a follower of Jesus Christ through all this?

In other words, what are you going to be and do as you mature?

Because God's will for your life encompasses all of these areas (and many, many more), you must depend on him to disclose what he wants you to be and do. So, what can you do to know God's will for your life?

Know God Personally

I am convinced that being who we are made to be as image-bearers of God is key to knowing his will. Remember: God created us in his image so that we, like a mirror, would reflect him in the world in which we live. This involves understanding and imitating God's communicable attributes. We are to be people of knowledge, wisdom, power, love, holiness, righteousness, jealousy, truthful-ness, faithfulness, sovereignty, mercy, grace, and godly wrath. We then are to reflect God in the world in which we live. The world in which you live is the network of relationships—at school, in your family, in the community, and at church—that you experience now. In the future, that world will change. It could include the world of business, teaching, raising children, missions, politics, social work, homemaking, sports, computers, media, the church, and so forth—but it will always be the world in which you live. This is and always will be your responsibility—to reflect God in the world in which you live. Your world may be very, very small—perhaps the little town in which you are now being raised. Your world may be very, very large—you could become a university professor, a judge for the circuit court of appeals, the mayor of a city, the CEO of a large corporation, a gold-medal-winning Olympic athlete, the president of an overseas missionary organization, or a cabinet member in the federal government. In any case, God's will is for you to reflect him in the world in which you live.

Worship God

Another way of knowing God's will is to worship him regularly and passionately. It is often during times of intense worship that God reveals what he wants us to do. A biblical example of this is the calling of the first Christian missionaries. It took place among a group of believers in the church of Antioch: "As they were ministering to the Lord and fasting, the Holy Spirit said, 'Set apart for Me Barnabas and Saul for the work that I have called them to.' Then, after they had fasted, prayed, and laid hands on them, they sent them off" (Acts 13:2–3). These early Christians sensed God's will as they engaged in intense worship.

It makes sense that God would clearly direct like this at times when we are seriously seeking him and praising him. I distinctly remember one particularly intense time of worship when God clearly directed me concerning his future will. The impressions of what God wanted to do with our ministry were so specific that I was able to write them down. Years later I looked back at that list and noted how God had accomplished those plans through our missionary work.

Because worship is such an important topic, I'll say more about it in the next chapter.

Acknowledge God as Father

An important step in knowing God's will is to realize that God wants to direct us because we are his children. Far too many Christians think that God takes pleasure in keeping us in the dark about his will. They picture him as a stingy, tightfisted miser who only begrudgingly offers his guidance. But what loving father intentionally withholds from his children the knowledge of what he wants them to do? He would be an evil father, and God is not at all like that. Rather, he promises that if we seek him by faith and depend on him to guide us, he will indeed direct the course of our lives:

> Trust in the LORD with all your heart
> and lean not on your own understanding;
> in all your ways acknowledge him,
> and he will make your paths straight. (Proverbs 3:5–6)

Indeed, God is eager for us to ask him for wisdom as we face the many choices in life: "If any of you lacks wisdom, he should ask God, who gives to all generously and without criticizing, and it will be given to him. But let him ask in faith without doubting" (James 1:5–6).

The God to whom we pray is ready to give us abundant wisdom, and he never criticizes us for turning to him for guidance. The only condition we must meet is that we trust that God will indeed give us the wisdom we need and seek.

Pray for Direction

Because God desires to guide us, we should expect that he will reveal his will as we seek his direction through prayer. This expectation

- should energize our prayers for understanding his will. As we pray, we should realize that the request "God, what do you want me to do?" pleases God and is heard by him.
- should encourage us to listen attentively for him to answer when we ask him to make his will known to us. As we pray, we should make sure to observe periods of silence for listening to and hearing what God wants to say to us.
- should motivate us to be sensitive to impressions from God. As we pray, then, we should expect to sense God's guidance. We shouldn't expect an audible voice, but this sense could be anything from a strong impression to a calm assurance that what we have in mind to do for God is truly his will.
- should encourage us to seek out counsel from more mature believers who know us intimately and can offer their wisdom in discerning God's will. It is especially important to check out personal impressions with other wise Christians for confirmation or questioning. Before we embark on something foolish or disastrous, asking "I have a strong sense that God is leading me in this direction—what do you think?" is a prudent and mature move.

 Let me tell you about the best advice I never took! I was at a crossroads in my life, and I was trying to discern God's will. Actually, a proposal for an overseas ministry had been made, and I was seriously considering if it was what God wanted me to do. I sought out a dear friend who was very wise and who had much experience in helping people discover God's direction. After I explained the proposal to him, he encouraged me to travel overseas to the place of ministry, stay there several weeks to observe the situation, and then see if I was the right person for the position. His counsel made a lot of sense to me, but because the flight would be expensive and the time commitment to investigate the situation would be fairly lengthy, I decided not to take his advice. I concluded it was God's will to take the position, so I accepted the proposal without checking it out further. Big mistake! I definitely was not the right person for the job, and after a year I saw the ministry collapse in front of my eyes. And this was only one of the many problems I encountered!

A word to the wise: Don't make the same mistake I did. If you are wise, seriously consider the advice of wise people in determining God's will for your life.

Read the Bible

Seeking God's will through reading his Word is obviously an important part of getting clear direction from him. I would discourage the dangerous practice of randomly opening the Bible and telling God that whatever you read next, you will take to be his guidance. Rather, I would suggest two ways to approach the Bible. The first is to begin or continue to read the Word every day. This may involve following a calendar that keeps you on track in your reading (some calendars have you read through the entire Bible in one year), or you may devise your own program. The importance of this kind of reading is to immerse yourself in the biblical worldview so as to gain a deeper sense of how God works and leads his people.

As you become more and more familiar with Scripture, the second approach comes into play. Consult specific portions of the Bible that you know will provide the kind of direction you need at specific periods in your life. For example, perhaps you are struggling with relationships within your family. Ephesians 6:1–4 and Colossians 3:20–21 will provide good direction. Perhaps you are sick and tired of the gossip and backbiting going on in your youth group, and you want help to stop it. James 3:1–12 will instruct you. Perhaps you and your friends disagree over activities like playing video games and hanging out at the arcade, wearing certain kinds of clothes and using more or less makeup, and so forth. Some of you think one way, others think a different way, and the Bible doesn't seem to take a stance. Reading Romans 14 will give you a good perspective. With time and experience, you will become more and more familiar with which passages in the Bible will provide solid help for you to deal with specific issues at different times.

As you read the Bible, God makes his will known in several different ways. At times, the Word explicitly states what God's will is. For example, Paul says: "For this is God's will, your sanctification: that you abstain from sexual immorality" (1 Thessalonians 4:3). It can't get much clearer than this! We are to be holy and, more specifically, we should be sexually pure. If you read this verse while you are involved in sexual immorality, you should understand that what you are doing violates God's will and deeply grieves him. Therefore, you should stop it immediately.

Not all directions about God's will, however, come as statements with the tag line "this is God's will." Many others take the form of commands. For example: "With every prayer and request, pray at all times in the Spirit, and stay alert in this, with all perseverance and intercession for all the saints" (Ephesians 6:18). God's will is that we attentively and continuously pray at all times in all circumstances in all ways for all Christians. This isn't a statement of God's will, but a command that confronts us with God's will and demands that we obey what he says. We sense the force of such a command; we feel compelled to pray.

Still another way that God makes his will known in Scripture is through stories. By drawing us into the lives of their characters and the drama they unfold, biblical stories are particularly effective ways of communicating God's will. For example:

- Exodus 32 recounts the story of the golden calf. Impatient with Moses, the Israelites melt down their gold jewelry and fashion an idol in the form of a calf. They put the golden calf on an altar and worship it by holding a wild party.
- Numbers 25 tells the story of some Israelites who engage in sexual immorality with pagan women and then begin to worship their idols. As punishment, God sends a terrible plague to kill thousands of Israelites.
- Numbers 21 relates the story of the Israelites' rebellious complaining against God. As punishment, God sends venomous snakes to bite the people and kill many of them.
- Numbers 16 is another story of grumbling against God that results in the destruction of thousands of people.

In his letter to the Corinthians, Paul uses these four stories to teach the people about God's will. He concludes: "Now these things became examples for us, so that we will not desire evil as they did. Don't become idolaters as some of them were; as it is written, 'The people sat down to eat and drink, and got up to play.' Let us not commit sexual immorality as some of them did, and in a single day twenty-three thousand people fell dead. Let us not tempt Christ as some of them did, and were destroyed by snakes. Nor should we complain as some of them did, and were killed by the destroyer. Now these things happened to them as examples, and they were written as a warning to us, on whom the ends of the ages have come" (1 Corinthians 10:6–11). As we read about the disobedience of the Israelites and the awful punishment that God brings against them, we, too, are warned not to follow their disastrous example. If we read these stories and we ourselves are currently involved in idolatry, sexual immorality, rebellion, or complaining against God, we sense what a dangerous space we are in. Being warned not to continue down our wrong path, we cease these activities and turn back to God. This is his will made known through these biblical stories.

Explicit statements of God's will. Commands setting forth God's will. Stories portraying God's will. As we read the Bible to discover God's will, we should be attentive to the various ways that his Word makes that will known to us.

Doing God's Will

When God makes his will known to us, his expectation is that we respond by doing it. Sometimes our response to God is to trust him with a particular situation. For example, I recall an incident in which I suspected that the whole truth wasn't being told. The person who was withholding information gained an advantageous position—she could save a lot of money but didn't really qualify for the financial break. I was very angry at this apparent injustice and was ready to blow the whistle on the deception.

But then I remembered this instruction: "Everyone must be quick to hear, slow to speak, and slow to anger, for man's anger does not accomplish God's righteousness" (James 1:19–20). I realized that if I responded to this situation with anger and made a phone call to expose the apparent falsehood, I would not accomplish God's will in the way it was to be done. Until I could deal with the situation in a proper way, I just had to trust God that he would right the wrong.

As it turned out, the person had not withheld information; an error had been made on someone else's part. Once the mistake was realized, the problem was corrected and no one was blamed for any wrongdoing. What a disaster I would have caused had I acted prematurely with anger! By trusting God, however, his will was accomplished in a constructive way.

Is God's will that you trust him with a particular situation at this time?

Sometimes our response is to obey God in a particular way. One of the most difficult things for me to do is say no to others. When others ask me to do something, I want to please them and find that I can't refuse their request—even when I know I don't have time to do it. More often than not, I end up saying yes. Then I don't do what they ask, or I do it poorly, disappointing both them and myself. I become angry with them for daring to ask me to help—after all, they should know I'm a busy person and not ask in the first place! I realize that saying yes to others means that I have to say no to other things—like my family, or myself—and that is not right. So I promise myself that I will say no in the future to these requests—but I violate that promise the very next time I say yes.

The Bible confronts this area of my life and demands my obedience. Jesus himself and the apostle James command, "Let your word 'yes' be 'yes,' and your 'no,' be 'no'" (Matthew 5:37; also see James 5:12). I realize that I cannot say yes to others when I have no intention of doing what they ask me to do. It is better to disappoint them with an initial response of no than to disappoint them later by not doing what I committed myself to do. The key is to tell them no graciously, without making them feel badly because they asked me. For example, I can honestly tell them that I would like to help them, but because of other commitments, I must say no. I may even be able to help them think of someone else whom they could ask instead of me. God's will for me to mean what I say demands a response of obedience on my part. Specifically, it takes the form of saying no to the requests of others when I know those requests are not in line with God's plan for my life at the time.

Is God's will that you obey him in a particular way at this time?

Sometimes our response is to praise and thank God for a particular gift. Sometimes it is to love God more passionately. Sometimes it is to reach out with love to those around us. You will experience many other ways to respond to God. The key is this: when God makes his will known, we must respond appropriately.

Doing God's Will in All Things

At times, we can get so caught up in focusing on the big issues of life that we fail to appreciate the daily journey of walking with God and doing his will in the everyday rhythm of life. The following lines in a song express what I mean:

I get so distracted by my bigger schemes
Show me the importance of the simple things
Like a word, a seed, a thorn, a nail
and a cup of cold water.[1]

Sure, it is right to be concerned about the important matters of life. These should be the focus of much prayer, counsel with others, searching the Word, and waiting on God. But we should never become so absorbed with these big issues that we neglect the smaller matters—visiting a grandparent, stopping in the hall to see how an unpopular student is doing, taking time off for a walk in the park, completing our household tasks in a timely manner, putting up with grief from a sibling without causing a major uproar at home, taking care to do homework well. These may seem like trivial matters, and in many cases they are. But as we've seen, our God is not only concerned about the big issues, he is also the God of the details. Living for him moment by moment as we follow his will is no mundane task. Rather, the dignity and significance with which God created us mean that each decision to trust him, each act of obedience, each prayer of thanks, each expression of praise, and each work of love pleases him. Enjoy the journey!

Finally, always remember who God is—the one whose will it is we desire to know and follow. He is wise, powerful, loving, and sovereign. Because the God who guides us in his will is wise, he always chooses the best goals and the best ways to accomplish those goals. Because the God who directs us in his will is powerful, he will never fail to provide the necessary resources for us to accomplish his will. Indeed, God's provisions to do his will are never merely adequate, for the Word explains that he "is able to do above and beyond all that we ask or think—according to the power that works in you" (Ephesians 3:20). Because the God who guides us is loving, we never have to doubt that his will for us is good. And because the God who directs us is sovereign, he will certainly accomplish all his good will and bring great glory to himself.

 Think through an area in which you are trying to discover God's will for your life and apply the ideas of this chapter that will help you further the process.

God's Quest for Authentic Worshipers

Sometimes I find myself completely into worshiping God. I strongly sense his presence and am fully focused on him, giving him honor for his greatness and goodness. Then there are those other times—because of tiredness, boredom, a broken relationship, a mind that just won't focus—that fall far short of what I want worship to be.

I recall one of those experiences of really engaging God in worship. The worship band was particularly excellent that Sunday morning. I was able to put aside the normal distractions and completely focus on God. But more importantly, the song we were singing gripped me. It was based on a vision that Isaiah the prophet had of God (Isaiah 6:1–9):

I saw the Lord seated on a throne, high and exalted, and the train of his robe filled the temple. Above him were seraphs, each with six wings: With two wings they covered their faces, with two they covered their feet, and with two they were flying. And they were calling to one another:

"Holy, holy, holy is the LORD Almighty;
the whole earth is full of his glory."

At the sound of their voices the doorposts and thresholds shook and the temple was filled with smoke.

It was this vision of God that captivated me that Sunday. He is the Lord Almighty, the Master—absolutely powerful, the Creator and Ruler of all people, the entire universe, and all that exists and takes place in it. As King over everything, he is seated symbolically on a throne—for ancient kings, the place of authority and power—from which he sovereignly rules and commands. As Lord, he is high and exalted—the spatial dimension pictures God as lifted up above everything else, raised up above all human authorities and angelic powers. Nothing can ever compare with him in majesty—he is absolutely unique, awesome in perfection, stunning in beauty, overwhelmingly glorious.

Strange flying creatures called seraphs—probably angelic-like beings—surround our exalted God. Together, the seraphs repeat a chorus of praise:

"Holy, holy, holy is the Lord Almighty;
the whole earth is full of his glory."

They recognize and proclaim that our God is absolutely holy—exalted above everything else and perfectly pure. So holy is he that the glory that radiates from him fills the entire world with its splendor. The intensity of the seraphs' praise is so great that its reverberations shake the temple—the decibel level is so high that it rocks the place of God's presence. And the temple itself is filled with smoke—our God is an all-consuming fire whose very presence destroys anything that falls short of his perfection.

No wonder Isaiah has the following reaction when he sees God in this vision: "'Woe to me!' I cried. 'I am ruined! For I am a man of unclean lips, . . . and my eyes have seen the King, the LORD Almighty!'" (v. 5). In the presence of our mighty, holy God, there can be no other cry than one of complete desperation. Who could ever stand before our exalted King? Who could ever come into the presence of our all-powerful Lord with the imperfections and sins that weigh us down? To capture a vision of God—or, better, to be captivated by such a vision—leaves us with an overwhelming sense of inadequacy to ever hope we could enjoy such a perfect and pure God.

Yet there is hope for us, as Isaiah himself found out: "Then one of the seraphs flew to me with a live coal in his hand, which he had taken with tongs from the altar. With it he touched my mouth and said, 'See, this has touched your lips; your guilt is taken away and your sin atoned for'" (vv. 6–7). A fiery coal symbolized for Isaiah our holy God's act of grace to cleanse him from his sin. God alone can forgive us and remove the guilt that we have accumulated by our wrong thoughts and evil acts. Being full of mercy, God himself comes to our rescue and restores us to a place of friendship with him.

Enjoying a relationship of grace and forgiveness with our holy God changes us and everything about us. Isaiah was aware of this, as he completed his account of his vision of God: "Then I heard the voice of the LORD saying, 'Whom shall I send? And who will go for us?' And I said, 'Here am I. Send me!'" (v. 8).

Knowing God through an experience of his mercy opens our senses and makes us ready to respond to him with trust and obedience. Isaiah heard God pleading for someone to serve him. Isaiah became that someone, offering his life to serve the Lord. For anyone who is gripped with a vision of God through worship, life takes on new meaning. The worship of our holy, exalted Lord changes us in a radical way. We become faithful and obedient to him. This is exactly how God himself designed us, his image-bearers, to be.

PAUSE TIME——I want to give you a final challenge. Perhaps you are expecting me to urge you to worship God more faithfully and passionately than you have in the past. That would be a good idea, and I hope that this book has given you much for which you can worship God. Yes, God is worthy of our honor and praise, so worship him as you've never done before.

But that isn't my final challenge. Rather, I want you to be amazed by something Jesus Christ says: "Yet a time is coming and has now come when the true worshipers will worship the Father in spirit and truth, for they are the kind of worshipers the Father seeks" (John 4:23 NIV).

Jesus tells us that God himself seeks people to worship him! This book, as part of the *TruthQuest* series, is supposed to be about our quest for God. But now Jesus tells us about another quest—God's quest for authentic worshipers. Why the Father would search for us to worship him is a mystery beyond understanding. But I do know this—as people created in his image, God seeks for us to worship him.

So do God's will. Please him. Worship him faithfully and passionately—not only because he is the only one worthy of our honor and praise, but also because he seeks for you to be his authentic worshiper.

Credits

Many people and resources have contributed to the development of my theology, but none more than my good friend Wayne Grudem. Much of the material in chapters 4, 6, 7, 8, and 9 reflects this influence and its expression in his book *Systematic Theology: An Introduction to Biblical Doctrine* (Leicester: InterVarsity and Grand Rapids: Zondervan, 1994).

Notes

Chapter 1

1. "Evidence of God," Geoff Moore/Roscoe Meek, © 1995 Songs On The Forefront/SESAC/Starstruck Music/ASCAP, all rights administered by EMI Christian Music Publishing, used by permission.

Chapter 3

1. *Westminster Shorter Catechism,* question 4, in Philip Schaff, *The Creeds of Christendom,* volume 3: *The Evangelical Protestant Creeds* (Grand Rapids: Baker, 1931), 676–77.

Chapter 5

1. "Big Enough," Chris Rice, © 1998 Clumsy Fly Music, from the album *Past the Edges* released by Rocketown Records, used by permission.

Chapter 7

1. "Chorus of Faith," Michael Card/Phil Naish, © 1994 Birdwing Music/Davaub Music/ASCAP, all rights administered by EMI Christian Music Publishing, used by permission.

2. "Breathe," Marie Barnett, © 1995 Mercy/Vineyard Publishing, all rights reserved, used by permission.

Chapter 8

1. *Nicene-Constantinople Creed* (A.D. 381) with the addition of *filioque* ("and the Son") by the Synod of Toledo (A.D. 589), in Philip Schaff, *The Creeds of Christendom,* volume 2: *The Greek and Latin Creeds* (Grand Rapids: Baker, 1931), 59.

Chapter 9

1. Michael Behe, *Darwin's Black Box* (New York: Touchstone, 1996), 42–43.

Chapter 10

1. Adapted from D. A. Carson, *How Long, O Lord?: Reflections on Suffering and Evil* (Grand Rapids: Baker, 1990), 201.

Chapter 11

1. Mary Baker Eddy, *Science and Health with Key to the Scriptures* (Boston: The First Church of Christ, Scientist, 1994), 480 (23, 24).

2. David Hume, *Dialogues Concerning Natural Religion,* part 10, in *The Empiricists* (New York: Anchor Books Doubleday, 1990), 490.

3. Adapted from John Feinberg, *The Many Faces of Evil* (Grand Rapids: Zondervan, 1994), 347–48.

Chapter 12

1. C. S. Lewis, *The Problem of Pain* (New York: Macmillan, 1962), 93.

Chapter 13

1. "The Power of a Moment," Chris Rice, © 1998 Clumsy Fly Music, from the album *Past the Edges* released by Rocketown Records, used by permission.